HOLDING ON

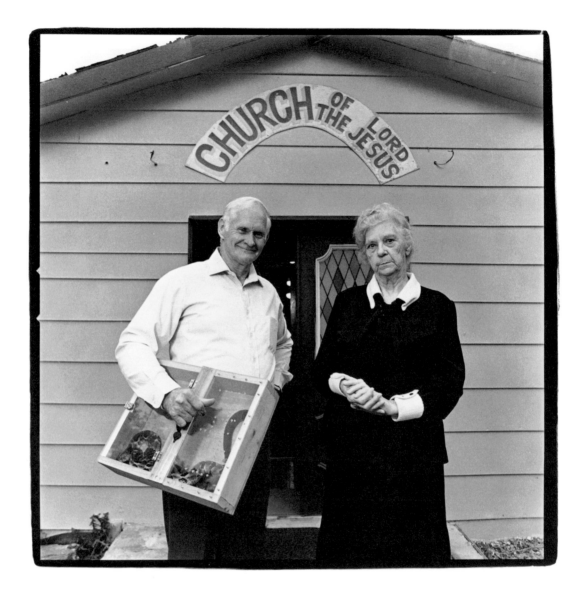

HOLDING ON

David Isay

Photographs by Harvey Wang

W·W·Norton & Company

New York   London

The text of this book is composed in 11/14.5 Electra

with the display set in Latino Elongated at 120% horizontal scale

Manufacturing by Becotte & Gershwin

Book design by Margaret M. Wagner

As sponsor of the traveling exhibition "Holding On," Philip Morris Companies Inc. celebrates the unusual, but yet remarkable, American traditions that should not be soon forgotten and are documented here with passion and insight. Philip Morris has funded the arts since 1958, with a focus on the visual and performing arts in the communities in which the company operates.

Library of Congress Cataloging-in-Publication Data

Wang, Harvey.

Holding on: dreamers, visionaries, eccentrics, and other American

heroes / photographs by Harvey Wang; text by David Isay.

p. cm.

1. United States—Social life and customs—1971- 2. United

States—Biography. I. Isay, David. II. Title.

E169.04.W356 1995

973.92—dc20   95-15724

ISBN 0-393-03754-1

W. W. Norton & Company, Inc., 500 Fifth Avenue, New York, N.Y. 10110

W. W. Norton & Company Ltd., 10 Coptic Street, London WC1A 1PU

1 2 3 4 5 6 7 8 9 0

This book is dedicated to the men and women it celebrates.

Contents

Foreword

BY HENRY ROTH

It seems to me that in my case, the return to creativity was not a question of doggedly holding on, so much as it was a process which doggedly wouldn't let go. I imagine that hanging on to a high-voltage wire must be something like that. The current is killing you, but you can't get rid of it—except by converting yourself, figuratively speaking, into a vehicle for discharging the immense store of static electricity you've accumulated over the years. You're old, possibly doddering, and like myself approaching the end. You're approaching the end, no matter what you do—or don't do—but at least you're not being destroyed by resisting the one force within you, the creative force, that seeks an outlet which you can provide.

My feeling has always been that I owe my fellow human beings, my fellow sufferers; I owe them a helping hand. I owe them a helping hand in whatever form I can extend it. While I'm alive I feel an obligation to exercise the long-dormant (or repressed) talent I have—in my case, writing. To me it's an exercise in decency and humanity. It probably does me good too, gives me an incentive, a goal, mitigates the misery inherent in these pitiless eighties and nineties.

Since I'm not a religious man, that's the way I feel. But whether you're religious or not, the photos and stories in *Holding On*, of people who still exercise their powers of creativity, their artistic or collector's or storytelling skills, and don't shirk what they're still capable of doing—they're all my brothers and sisters regardless of origin and upbringing, because in doing what they do they affirm the positive values of mankind. They oppose despair at the sad state of the world with the dignity and decency of creativity. They lend their fellow sufferers a helping hand. In that sense we're kinfolk, we belong to a special club, a special society: people who ease the time for everybody, including themselves. And who knows? By their example they may modify for the better the time to come, may modify for the better the behavior of future generations.

What I'm trying to say is not preachment; it's common sense. You either rust with disuse, grow musty with stagnation. Or, if you've got a feeling there's something you're endowed with the talent to accomplish, doing so (or even trying to do so) will make the inevitable remnant of life a little easier to bear.

I guess this is all I have to say. Our eyes will close forever soon enough. And even if you don't believe in a hereafter, you don't believe a thing, don't close them while they're still open, while you can still see. Don't let the high voltage kill you if you can still convert it into a conduit for communication with your fellow humans. The least it does is help pass the time. It may make you feel better. But it does a lot more: exercising creativity helps us preserve one of our proudest, most noble, most precious possessions: *dignity*. As far as I'm concerned, dead, it doesn't matter whether we did or didn't preserve it. Comes to the same thing. "Golden lads and girls all must, as chimney-sweepers, come to dust," says the supreme bard, William Shakespeare. We're talking about being alive.

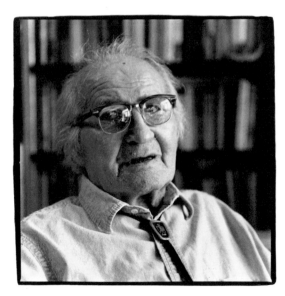

Author Henry Roth suffered one of literature's most famous and profoundly agonizing cases of writer's block. After publication of the classic novel Call It Sleep *in 1934, nearly sixty years passed before Roth published his next novel,* A Star Shines over Mt. Morris Park.

Preface

It was probably sometime toward the end of 1988 that I first walked into the offices of City Lore in New York. I'd just started doing freelance radio pieces for National Public Radio, and had already settled into something of a niche, producing audio profiles of offbeat characters around the city. I'd heard that City Lore was a clearinghouse of information about these sorts of folks, and indeed it was. At the end of the visit the organization's director, Steve Zeitlin, told me about someone he thought I might like: a photographer named Harvey Wang. He went into a file and pulled out a list Harvey compiled, which I have before me now, tacked to my bulletin board. It's computer-printed, several pages long. Each page contains the names and occupations of dozens of New Yorkers in no apparent order: Pete Benfaremo—LEMON ICE KING, Martha Gronsky—POLAR BEAR CLUB, Joe Baffi—BOXING TRAINER, George Williams—SELTZER DISTRIBUTOR . . . More than a hundred of them: pool parlor owners, milk men, ballroom dance instructors, TV repairmen, gravediggers, pawnbrokers, elevator operators. I was ecstatic! I doubt Harvey would have approved, but I managed to talk Steve out of a copy of the list. I knew I'd found a soul mate. I called Harvey to tell him, but he wasn't convinced.

For several months I pestered Harvey, and he did his best to hustle me off the phone. It took a while, but he eventually warmed up. A wonderful book of his photographs, *Harvey Wang's New York*, was published in 1990, and I jumped at the chance to produce a piece about it for *Weekend All Things Considered*. It was the first time Harvey and I had met face-to-face. I'd just gotten funding from the Corporation for Public Broadcasting to produce *The American Folklife Radio Project*, a national version of the sorts of stories I'd been producing around New York. We decided that day to collaborate on a book.

Originally we set out to create a book similar to Harvey's first—documenting vanishing traditions and trades across the country. A few months into the project, though, we took a look at the material we'd gathered and decided to shift our focus. Harvey and I both found ourselves drawn toward particular types of subjects. Eccentrics, visionaries, dreamers, believers: men and women in pursuit of *something*, and holding on to that at all costs. These were stories of sacrifice, of quiet heroism, of obsession. There seemed to be certain qualities shared by all of the subjects, but we couldn't pin them down. Was it the sense of loneliness? The bravery? Individuality? Resilience? Was it that oddly wistful feeling we were left with each time we visited one of these people? While driving a long stretch of west Texas highway one day we decided to quit worrying about definitions. We realized there was just a single, simple criterion we'd been using all along for inclusion in this book: these were all people we'd fallen in love with.

Harvey and I spent more than three years gathering material for this book. Sometimes I'd head out first to do the radio stories with Harvey following a month or two later. Sometimes we'd travel together, Harvey standing by patiently while I recorded my piece, waiting for an opportune time to make a portrait with his Hasselblad. There were plenty of difficult moments on the road, to be sure: tire blowouts in the middle of the desert, a nearly broken ankle while serpent-hunting in the rattlesnake-infested hills of West Virginia, miserable, all-night drives, motel rooms where you have to screw in the bulbs for light, and countless *truly* lousy meals. But when all was said and done, at the end of the day Harvey and I would invariably look at one another, exhausted and giddy, knowing without question that we had the greatest jobs in the world.

Acknowledgments

Holding On began as a radio series for NPR. For this, special thanks to Rick Madden from the Corporation for Public Broadcasting's Radio Program Fund; his faith and encouragement made this radio series and book possible. Also from CPB, thanks to Loretta Hobbs, Wendy Hoover, and Jennifer J. Parker. Thanks to my wonderful studio engineer Caryl Wheeler, series editor Jude Doherty, and Ellen Weiss, executive producer of *All Things Considered*. Thanks also to the various editors, producers, engineers, and other assorted radio characters who had a hand in getting these stories to air: Rob Rand, Jane Greenhalgh, Cindy Carpien, Steve Tripoli, Larry Abramson, Greg Allen, Melissa Block, Manoli Wetherell, David Goren, Neal Rauch, Preston Brown, Lance Neal, Andy Lyman, Art Silverman, Sara Sarasohn, Alex Chadwick, Sean Collins, Jean Durr, Sharon Green, John Guardo, Leslie Peters, Quincey Johnson, Charlotte Taylor, Lynn Neary, Bruce Drake, Bob Ferrante, Elisabeth Perez-Luna, Len Persky, Lars Hoel, Rob Robinson, Kee Malesky, Bill Craven, Bob Boilen, Bill Buzenberg, John Dinges, Merle Jawitz, Anna Maria Defrietas, Moira Rankin, Marie Dilg, Brooke Gladstone, Spyder Blue Rider, Bill Wax, Ellen McDonnell, Vicki O'Hara, Gene DeAnna, Wynn Matthias, and Tom Pack. Also to Michael Alcamo, for his legal advice and tireless efforts on behalf of Moreese Bickham. Special thanks to Bob Weil, Henry Roth's editor and a friend to this project from the beginning. Very special thanks to Steve Zeitlin of City Lore, who introduced me to Harvey, and was a constant source of support and story ideas throughout.

This book has been over three years in the making, and the writers, historians, folklorists, and others in all fifty states who've helped us find *Holding On* subjects are far too numerous to list. We're deeply indebted to all of you. Special thanks to: Ron and Kay Wikberg, Wilbert Rideau, Mark Young, Ken Smith, Jack Barth, Geneva Keene, Emily Benedek, Roger Manley, Michael Wallace, Chuck Woodbury, the Kansas Grass Roots Arts Association, Ann Ruff, Vincent Borrelli, Hampton Sides, Ken Driggs, Dorothy House, Jane Meggers, Suzanne Martin, Jill Sundby, Tarry Owens, Sam Malone, Jack Holzhueter, Joey Brackner, Steve Ohrn, Libby Sholes, Tom Leary, Mike Vogel, Bill Siener, Christopher Johns,

Connie Mays, John Tyson, Jose Mallea-Olaetxe, Linda White, Dick Zigun, Susan Slyomovics, Patty Johnson, Jim O'Neal, Tom Rankin, David Evans, Bill Ferris, Marcy Cohen, Emily Benedek, Dorothy House, Beatrice Norton, Salvador Rodríguez del Pino, Jim Salem, Steve Filmanowicz, Ann Parker, John Hahn, Scott Gorman, Don Bishoff, John Davenport, George Toomer, Renée Kientz, Jack McGuire, Larry Hodge, John L. Smith, Janet Miller, Ron Hoon, Mary Tolan, George Lee, Jens Lund, Mike Thoele, Keith Halperin, George Lee, Chris Brady, David Brose, Slim Randalls, Elisio Torres, Gary James, Pat Jasper, Erich John, Ben Salazar, and Roberta Singer. Thanks most of all to the mysterious Tony Shaia, by far our most prolific source, whose tireless obsession with the sorts of characters profiled in this book has never ceased to amaze us. Apologies to all of those we inevitably overlooked.

For encouragement, inspiration, and advice, many thanks to: Amy Goodman, Dan Pinkwater, Bev Donofrio, Gene Mahon, Bill Siemering, Jeanne Reilly, Susan Stamberg, Julie Cohen, Diana Halperin, Scott Lowell, the Wilker brothers, Jocelyn Meinhardt, Erica Meinhardt, Ben Katchor, Ren Weschler, Nancy Fish, Donna Gallers, Sandy Tolan, Ellen Baker, Calvin Roche, Maria Cabodecvilla-Conn, Charles Bender, Joe Katz, Leontien Ruttenberg, Rose and the Diner Boys, my radio mentor Gary Covino, my adopted brothers LeAlan Jones and Lloyd Newman as well as my adopted grandmother June Jones and the rest of the Jones and Newman families, my blood brother Josh Isay, my radio brother Dan Collison, Dick Isay, Gordon Harrell, and (of course) my mother, Jane Isay, who is still the first to read everything I write.

Finally, thanks to my assistant, Shelle Davis, for her infinite patience and invaluable help; my agent, Jonathan Dolger; from Norton, Tabitha Griffin, Ted Johnson, Margaret Wagner, Karen Auerbach, Louise Brockett, and most of all our editor Jim Mairs, who stuck by us for three years without blinking and showed me how to make this into a book.

Holding On *is adapted from* The American Folklife Radio Project, *which originally aired on National Public Radio. The series was funded with a major grant from the Corporation for Public Broadcasting. The book was written with the support of a John Simon Guggenheim Foundation Fellowship.*

Photographer's Acknowledgments

BY HARVEY WANG

Making *Holding On* was a journey across America. Seeking subjects, entering lives, making connections, taking pictures. It was also a journey of friendship and synchronicity with David Isay. David is a gifted interviewer, an inspired archivist, and a great collaborator. After months on the road, he is also a great friend.

As a photographer I labor to find, document, preserve, and interpret. Much of this work is a solitary exercise. Working on this book, I met many incredible people who labor out of the spotlight for a lifetime. I identify with the solitary nature of these pursuits and rejoice in the spirit that keeps these people alive.

So many people have been helpful and supportive of my work. I'd like to thank Alan Kaufman for his support, Florence Sillen for her patience and faith, Julia Mayo for her counsel, David Shayat of the Smithsonian Institution for exhibiting this work, Rob Maass and Richard Sandler for their friendship and critiques, Isa Brito for assisting with the prints, and my parents, Edna and Leo Wang. Meeting Henry Roth was one of the highlights of my travels, and I am thrilled that he introduces the book.

I've had the great fortune to work with Jim Mairs, my editor at W. W. Norton whose decision to publish *Harvey Wang's New York* (1990) has allowed me to continue doing the work that I love. Thanks for his continued encouragement. I am grateful for the support of Karen Broscius, Jennifer Goodale, Keiko Hayes, and Philip Morris Companies Inc. And also for the assistance of Peggy Mahoney and Contenental Airlines, Fuji Photo Film USA, and Steve Zeitlin of City Lore.

Thanks to Sonja Sohn, my mate and collaborator in life—I love you. And my girls, Sakira and Sophia, the brightest stars in my life.

HOLDING ON

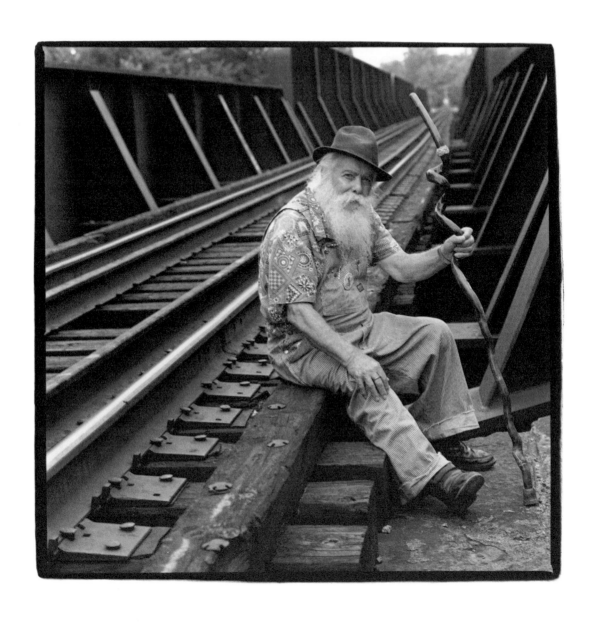

"Steam Train" Maury Graham

HOBO

LOGANSPORT, INDIANA

I met "Steam Train" Maury Graham while recording a story about the National Hobo Convention in August 1992. The town of Britt, Iowa, has hosted the annual three-day gathering since 1900, when some locals decided that the convention might help the quiet town to grow a bit. The town never grew, and the hoboes never stopped coming. They continue to descend on Britt each year—camping out next to the railroad tracks. The 1992 convention drew about sixty wandering souls—most of them younger drifter types, heavy on the tattoos and Harley-Davidson T-shirts, in search of a party. But there were also a fair number of Depression-era hoboes in attendance, most of whom had been coming to the convention for decades, a few of whom were still riding the rails. "Steam Train" Maury is now considered the hoboes' elder statesman and acts as master of ceremonies at most of the convention's events. Maury had suffered a stroke in 1991, and was unable to attend the previous year's convention. At the 1992 convention he was greeted with a hero's welcome.

I'm "Steam Train" Maury, Graham is my last name, and I'm seventy-five years old. I spent many years traveling around the country on freight trains and working. I first went on the road when I was thirteen years old. I had a broken home, so I just took off. Luckily, I got in a camp of old hoboes in Toledo, Ohio. They tried to encourage me to get home—they don't like kids hanging around their camp. I brought them some vegetables, so they let me stay a little while and they taught me the ways of the hobo. They told me the difference between hoboes and bums, and they said: "You go in those bum camps and you might not come out of there, 'cause they'll rob you and they'll hit you in the head. But if you stay around the hoboes, they'll look out for you and they'll treat you nice." I asked 'em, "How do you know a hobo?" Well, they start a-learnin' me. "You can tell the hobo by the way they're dressed, and you can tell the hobo by their conversation—usually not shady."

Also, they taught me little tricks, like always have a few pebbles in your pocket. If you come into a camp and there's a bunch of men you don't know, take one of those pebbles and throw it on the ground. All the men will know that you've been passed by the hobo clan and that you belong to them. So I would always carry a few little pretty stones, and just throw them on the ground when I come into the camp. Now if it was a bunch of bums, they don't even see me do that. But if it's a bunch of hoboes, they see that rock on the ground, and right away I'm under their wing, and I share their dinner and so on. I used to do that, and I'd be taken care of and looked after, and that was good for a kid thirteen years old.

There's two ways of thinking about how the hobo got his name, and two stories that come down through history. One is that hoboes could always get a job working in a garden. Everybody had gardens full of vegetables, and every day they'd need hoeing in the garden. The woman's hoe was usually dull and dirty and not handy to use, so the hobo started carrying his own hoe, and many of them carried a hoe over their shoulder: they'd tie their bedroll and all of their possessions onto the handle of their hoe, and carry it across their shoulder. They call it a bindle, B-I-N-D-L-E, and you carry everything in there. So the word started coming down, "Oh, there goes a boy with a hoe! There goes a hoe-boy." Well, the hobo started resenting being called a "boy"—a "hoe-boy"—and they'd let people know: "I'm an adult person—don't call me a boy!" And the vernacular for an adult was "bo," and it come from the old English "bo"—that's an adult man. And so they'd say, "There goes a ho-bo"—that's a *man* carrying a hoe—not a boy carrying a hoe. And that's where the word come from—hobo.

And another story that come down through history is that it was a salutation, like you'd say to a fellow you run across coming from the opposite direction, "Hi boy, where you going?" And he'd say, "I'm not a boy, I'm a man," and they'd start saying to them then, "Ho-bo, where you goin'?" 'Ho' was an old English expression of salutation—"Hello." "Ho-bo, where, you goin'? Ho-bo, where you been?" And they started calling them "hoboes."

There's several groups of people on the road. The biggest part of them is called 'bums', and they bum because they want something for nothing. They don't do any work in this world. If you just sit down and depend on people to give to you, that's a bum. If you bum people and beg people for something for nothing, that's a bum. Now, the hobo would never do that. He'd say: "I'm a class a little higher than that. Have you got any work I can do?" And trade work for something to eat. You didn't have to trade work for money then. There wasn't any money. You'd rather get a meal for the work, or you'd rather get a pair of pants or an overcoat or a blanket. Usually in the old times that's the way people paid the man—paid him in trade. You aim to work and that's a work ethic.

A hobo never worried about being broke. He knew he could work for his breakfast, and he knew he could work for his dinner. When you were hungry, you'd knock on a door and ask for work. And the housewife would either have some wood to carry in or wood to split, or coal to carry in and ashes to carry out. The husband was supposed to do that, but he didn't do it half the time, and they was glad that somebody come to the door to do it. And by feeding the hobo a meal, why they could get it done. And some housewives were very liberal and very generous and some of them were very skimpy and very tight. You might do two hours' work, and just get a little old peanut butter sandwich for it. But the biggest part of them were generous.

Where the hoboes eat and hang around and sleep under the stars—that's the "hobo jungle." Usually along a railroad track or out by a creek someplace. There's usually a collection of pots and pans there, so that they can cook some dinner. And when they get through using those pans, they wash 'em and clean 'em. They don't throw them on the ground and leave them dirty—bums do that. Hoboes wash and shine those pots and get them perfectly clean, and hang them upside down to dry on a stick so dirt won't drift into them. They're clean—ready for the next bunch to come in!

Many of the hoboes wrote little markers on a telephone post or a fence with chalk. They'd leave signs that meant: "This is a good place to turn in and get some work." And a good turn-in sign was a tic-tac-toe with an arrow pointing in. And a picture of an old top hat like Lincoln used to wear, that meant: "There's a good man living in here, and he's got work for you." And if there was a bad dog in there they'd put two jagged lines for two sets of teeth: "There's teeth in there! Don't go in!" It was usually a dog, but it could be a bad man, two jagged lines.

It was extremely dangerous—catching trains. A lot of it was hardship, so don't get too romantic about it. Many a man fell under the trains and was killed, and many a men had limbs cut off. Oh, the country was full of one-legged, one-armed men. And a lot of people died and a lot of men did get hurt, but I never did. It was a lot of hard knocks.

Those old days when men traveled to get work like that is over. The railroad people, they don't want you on their trains, wandering and wandering and wandering. And the towns down the line don't want you coming through, traveling and traveling. I'd say '79 was probably the last time I rode. I'm old and crippled, you know, and not strong like I used to be. One day I just said to myself, "You'll never do that again." But a lot of old men that are decrepit *do* stay out there and keep at it and keep at it. And a lot of men die out there. Just stay with it until they die. Yeah, it is hard to leave, but it's the smart thing to do. To stay home in a nice easy chair. I don't mind that. ■

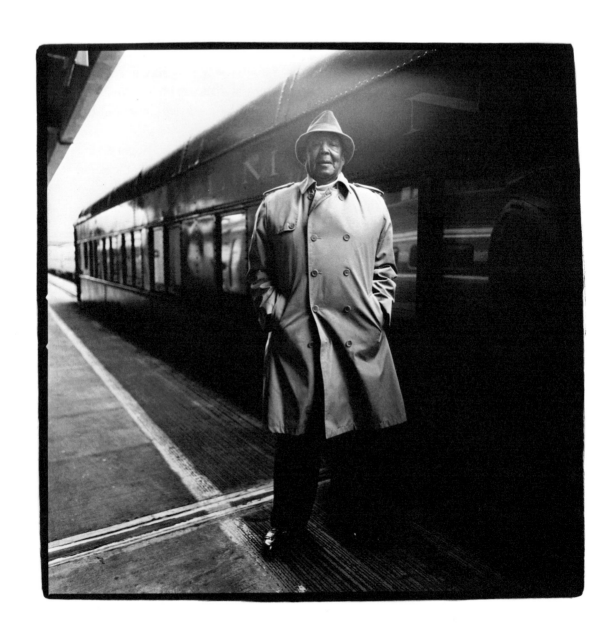

Lawrence W. "Happy" Davis
PULLMAN PORTER (RETIRED)
WASHINGTON, D.C.

In 1865, at the dawn of America's golden era of railroading, a designer named George Pullman created a "hotel on wheels"—a plush sleeper car, the likes of which had never before been seen. It was a huge success. By the turn of the century, the Pullman Palace Car Company had a monopoly on the sleeper business, operating first-class cars on all of the country's major railroads.

Pullmans quickly became an icon of American luxury—as famous for the service delivered on board as for the accommodations. All the cars were staffed by Pullman porters—African-American workers who greeted passengers, carried their luggage, made their beds, and shined their shoes. By the 1920s, the Pullman Company was the single largest private employer of African–Americans in the country.

The job offered these porters a mix of opportunity and indignity. While the men were able to make a relatively good living from their tips, they were always contending with racist passengers and conductors. The porters, who had to smile at all times or risk being fired, were usually called "George" after George Pullman, rather than by name. In 1925, under the leadership of A. Philip Randolph, the porters formed the Brotherhood of Sleeping Car Porters. When the union was finally recognized by the Pullman Company in 1937, it was the first labor agreement between a large American corporation and a union of black workers.

Along with the rest of American railroading, the Pullman Company went into a steep decline in the years after the Second World War, eclipsed by airplanes and superhighways. By the late 1960s, the era of the pullman porter had come to an end.

I had originally hoped to produce a radio documentary about the annual meeting of the Association of Retired Pullman Porters, a group I'd learned about from a wonderful documentary film by Paul Wagner and Jack Santino called "Miles of Smiles, Years of Struggle." By the time I got around to doing the piece in 1993, so many of the retired porters died that the organization had ceased meeting. I did manage to find about a dozen porters around the country, and decided to interview Happy Davis. I spoke with Mr. Davis in the dining room of his home in Washington, D.C. He talked for three hours straight. I barely asked a question.

My name is Lawrence W. Davis. They call me Happy for short. I was born December the 9th, 1908, in D.C. I worked for the Pullman Company from 1925 until I retired. When I first went to work for the Pullman Company, I put my age up—you know what I mean? I was eighteen. [Whispers] I put my age up to twenty. I know a lot of fellows who did that—and then they retired at the wrong age.

But when Social Security come, I straightened it up—I went back to the date I was really born, you see. You could do those things back there then.

The job per se was one of the greatest experiences a man could have. Being poor and never having been anywhere, the Pullman porter went all over the United States. I been to every bit of this country. Every bit of it! From Maine to California. Because back then, the railroad was it. Wasn't no planes. Very few cars, and buses were uncomfortable just like they are now. So the average American who had money—they put you on a Pullman. See, the Pullman was first-class. Pullman had some cars that was just like a palace!

A Pullman porter is a man, first of all, who makes beds. And the next thing he's a man who receives and takes care of passengers—clean up behind them, make them comfortable, make their beds, and make sure they get off at their proper destination. The Pullman porter was one of the greatest people sitters of all times—that's how I put it. Every day was something new. Every time you get on a Pullman car you was coming out for a different experience. You didn't know whom you was going to meet, you didn't know what was going to happen. I barnstormed with the Yankees, I barnstormed with the Brooklyn Dodgers. I had Miller Huggins, Babe Ruth, I had Musial, Wally Pip. I had a lot of the big bands—I had Count Basie and his band. And you know what? Everybody's the same—they're plain Joes, like you and I!

We wasn't getting paid much of anything, but we had a supplement to our pay: the great American public. Every time a porter climbed up on a car, people would give you any kind of tip. A Pullman porter should never have been broke. Never. Never! I raised seven children working for the Pullman Company. Can I call names? Peter Lawford—he would not tip a porter! Peter Lawford wouldn't give a porter a dime—he'd go out the back door on you every time! And Sammy Davis, Jr.—he's my buddy. That man paid. He paid! I guess I've had a great amount of experience out there with those people.

No two porters were alike. Wherever we were, you found a bunch of compatible men from all walks of life. It was the best job a Negro could get back then—you know what I mean? Most of us were well educated. We had doctors, lawyers, who took a job as a Pullman porter because they couldn't make a living out there. Oh yes, no question about that. That's a foregone conclusion. Dr. Tillis and I was just like that. We had ministers of the gospel out there, preachers. There was great camaraderie between us—we were comrades, all right.

The Brotherhood of Sleeping Car Porters was originally started in 1925. But it wasn't recognized until 1937. Before the Brotherhood you wasn't nothing. You was part of the equipment. Like a rug on the floor or something. Anybody could charge you with anything, reprimand you or do anything to you. A passenger would say, "He didn't smile at me." "He didn't shine my shoes last night." And that Pullman conductor, he'd make it rough for you if he didn't like you. But when the Brotherhood got strong, we didn't have that trouble no more. Thank God for A. Philip Randolph. The organization fought tooth and nail for us. They had to have bulldog tenacity to face the white man the way they did—you know what I mean? They faced one of the toughest companies. . . . The Pullman Company was stronger than the United States government, tell you the truth!

But after all is said and done, it was a good job for me. I enjoyed the railroad, I did. Up until that last four or five days, I never thought that last day would get you. And when the last day arrived, I was coming from Chicago. I pulled that uniform off, took a great big piece of rope out of one of them linen bags. Shoes and all, I rolled them up and I said, "Anybody want this uniform?" Nobody accepted it, so I threw that uniform in the Potomac River. [Laughs] No more working, no more uniform, no more nothing! Oh goodness, so many extra-ordinary experiences out there. Shucks, I couldn't reminisce enough to tell you all about 'em. I really couldn't. ■

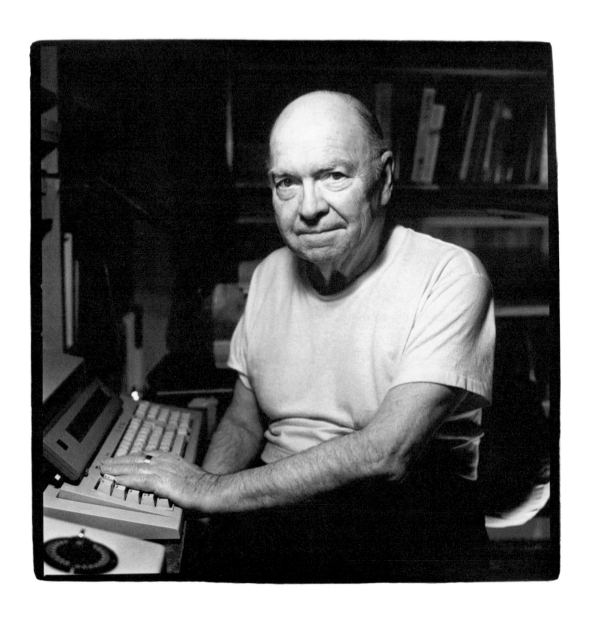

Robert Shields

AUTHOR, THE WORLD'S LONGEST DIARY
DAYTON, WASHINGTON

Several years ago, Harvey introduced me to a wonderful, rather eccentric eighty-year old gentleman in New York City named Edward Robb Ellis. For the past sixty-some years, without missing a day, Mr. Ellis had been keeping a diary of his life. When I met him, his diary was up to about nineteen million words. I understand that Mr. Ellis is still hard at work.

I produced a profile of Eddie Ellis in 1989, and was fairly certain that it would be my one and only "world's longest diary" story. Until I heard about Robert Shields. For the past twenty years, Mr. Shields has spent his days keeping a minute-by-minute record of his life. We met Mr. Shields in October 1993, when his diary was more than 34 million words long (34,263,395 words, to be precise — Mr. Shields is a stickler for detail).

Shields spends his days holed up in the small office off the back porch of his family's home, chained to his typewriter, recording everything that happens to him every moment of the day. He types his diary in two perfect columns down sheets of 11 x 14 paper, which he eventually binds into ledgers and stores in huge cartons, seventy-five of which are stacked to the ceiling in the hall just outside his office.

It was Halloween night, 1993, when Harvey and I descended on the Shields household, where Robert lives with his wife, Grace, and daughter Cornelia.

I'm Robert W. Shields, and I turned seventy-five last May. I'm a retired secondary school teacher, and an ordained minister of the United Church of Christ. I also do writing. I started twenty years ago, keeping a diary. Complete for twenty years. Every minute accounted for. What takes place, whether I'm sleeping or whether I'm awake. If I remember the dreams I put the dreams in. It's an *uninhibited* diary. Tell all, show all. I don't leave anything out. Here's the inventory for this past year: October 25th, 1992–October 25th, 1993. In one year I did 1,100,000 words. I used to do three to four million words a year, but I had a stroke two years ago and it slowed me down.

As far as I know, this is the longest diary in the history of the world. I start the diary each day by typing "GOD." That's "Genesis of the Day." Like today: From GOD–12:05: I peed. I read for a few moments from the Swedenborg Spiritual Diary, but I was too tired to take it in. 12:05–3:05: I slept nearly three hours. I dreamt, but the dream escapes me. 3:05–3:10: I discharged urine. 3:10–3:20: I was at the keyboard of my IBM Wheelwriter making entries for the diary. I took the four medications listed in the right hand margin: Lopressor: 50 mg;

Procardia: 60 mg; Trental: 400 mg; and aspirin. I took the readings given in the margins: Humidity 52°. Porch temperature 45°. Porch floor temperature 40°. Study temperature 77°. Door temperature in the study 74°. My hips ached, so I was bent over acutely and had to hold on to furniture to move about. . . .

Let me stop you for a second. You've taped something to the bottom of this page. . . .
That's nostril hair. For DNA purposes. In years to come they *might* be able to figure out my genetics from having a physical artifact.

And what's this?
Whenever I purchase anything like meat, particularly, I peel the stickers off and put it in the diary, because then there's a record of how much we bought and what the price of it was. I also put in calling cards, menus from restaurants—everything.

10:00–10:05	I groomed my hair with a scrub brush.
10:05–10:10	I fed the cat with tinned cat food.
10:10–10:20	I dressed in black Haband trousers, a pastel blue Bon Marché shirt, the blue Haband blazer with simulated silver buttons, both hearing aids, eyeglasses, and the 14° Masonic ring.
10:20–10:25	I tried to pick a spot of Krazy Glue off my black trousers that got on them yesterday. I was unsuccessful. Maybe it was Friday that I spotted them. I put a dab of liquid black shoe polish on the blemish and it helped some. . . .

How did this all start?
I had a diary back in high school and college, but it was just intermittent. Desultory. Then I thought: "Well, why not every minute of the day or night? Why not tabulate every minute?" That was 1972. Fall of that year. And it just kept going.

Why are you doing this?
It's an obsession, that's all I can say. It's an obsession. . . . I don't know. I really can't answer that. Sometimes I wonder why I impose it on myself, and then I say: "Well, I'd rather do this than do nothing." I want to be busy every minute of the day or night that I can be busy. If you're idle, that's a bad sign. It's not good to be

idle. It's my makeup. It's my nature, I suppose. I'm not boastful about it. It's just something that I do. Like an artist would do something, like an author would do something, like an architect would do something. So I do this. That's all.

How does your family feel about this?
Never asked them.

10:45		Grace and I left the house in the blue 1959 State Police Cruiser. The odometer on the 1959 Ford measures only .9 of a mile for every mile traveled.
10:48	97182.0	We left the post office after dispatching mail. It was 62°.
10:49	97182.4	We passed McQuary's Grocery at 301 Main Street, Dayton, WA 99328.
10:55	97187.1	We passed the entrance to Lewis and Clark Trail State Park. It was a sunny day, halcyon weather, summer skies.
11:00	97191.0	Denver Page's Waitsburg Chevron Station, 125 Preston Avenue.
11:09	97197.7	Summit of Minnick Hill. Jct. of the freeway with Lewis Peak Road.
11:11	97199.6	The middle of Dixie, Washington 99329 traversing a culvert.
11:15		Intersection of the Freeway with Spring Creek Road.
11:17		State Police Weighing Station. The scales were not in service today.
11:20	97207.2	Intersection of the Freeway with Spring Creek Road.
11:23	97207.8	The Prime Cut Restaurant, 1760 Isaacs.
11:29		I ordered a breaded fish filet and a baked potato, and Grace ordered a shish kebab. The fish was $1.99 and the shish kebab was $2.99. . . .

Do you read the diary?
No, 'cause if I read it I wouldn't have time to do anything else.

What about leaving town?
I don't leave town. I haven't left town since 1985. I don't like to be away overnight, because it gets me behind. If I travel to Walla Walla to do shopping it puts me behind in the diary. I have to take notes all the time, and when I get back

it takes me almost a day to catch up with the notes. So I avoid going out. I avoid being away. . . .

What happened when you had your stroke?
I kept handwritten notes in the hospital bed by the minute of every time the nurse came in or anytime I thought about anything. I was only three or four days in the hospital—it was a very light stroke—but it took me *days* to catch up.

12:20–12:25	I discharged urine.
12:25–12:30	I stripped to my thermals. I failed to mention that the *Tri City Herald* weighed in this morning at 1 lb., 11 1/2 ounces. It was the heaviest paper we have ever had to my knowledge, lacking only 1/2 oz. of being 1 3/4 lb. Think of that.
12:30–12:50	I ate leftover Bumble Bee Alaska red salmon, about seven ounces, while I guzzled 10 oz. orange juice and read the *Oxford Dictionary of Quotations.*
12:50–1:45	I was at the keyboard of my IBM Wheelwriter making entries for my diary. . . .
1:45–2:00	I picked up the dining room table so Grace could prepare dinner for Dave Isay and Harvey Wang. I put things away. I washed my hands. . . .

We've been sitting talking here for about forty-five minutes. Does that make you nervous?
No, no. I've got it caught up to four-thirty today, and I know what's happened since.

Do you feel like the diary controls you?
I feel like I'm in control. I could stop it at any time.

What would it do to you if you just stopped?
It would be like turning off my life.

6:10–6:15	Dave Isay and Harvey Wang arrived. I told them to park the car in the driveway, and we shut the gate. It was Halloween night and there is no use in taking any chances.

6:15–6:20   I showed them my 1959 Ford Washington State Patrol Car. I lifted the overhead door on the garage and they went in. I have a ceiling light in there.

6:20–6:30   Harvey set up his camera (a Hasselblad) in the study, and Dave Isay set up his recording mechanism. They wanted to be in the room where I worked.

6:30–8:35   The first thing was that Dave detected a hum. I was not aware of it, but it turned out to be the electric baseboard heater. We turned it off. The bathroom heater kept us warm enough. We left the door to the bathroom open. He had a great many questions written down. I could not answer some of them: Why did I write the diary? What started me? Did the inspiration come suddenly at a distinct time to keep it? (It did not, but developed in 1972.) Did I keep any unusual artifacts in the record outside of nasal hairs? (I kept the nasal hairs for DNA purposes in the hope that they would reveal something about my genetics.) He had me read through my diary for today, noting the times, and examining the format and the content for a week back. He wondered if any one was reluctant to talk to me for fear it would wind up in the diary. I said, very rarely, not as often as once every three or five years. He was amazed at the extensiveness of it and how neatly it was kept. It is a total record, covering or accounting for every minute of the day and night. . . . I said I did not know why I kept it, especially since it is doubtful if anyone would ever read it. It was a compulsion. He asked whether I intended to keep it up until I die and I said, Yes. It is impossible for me to give any motivation for it, except that when I am gone, the words that I have written will be the only thing that survives. . . . ■

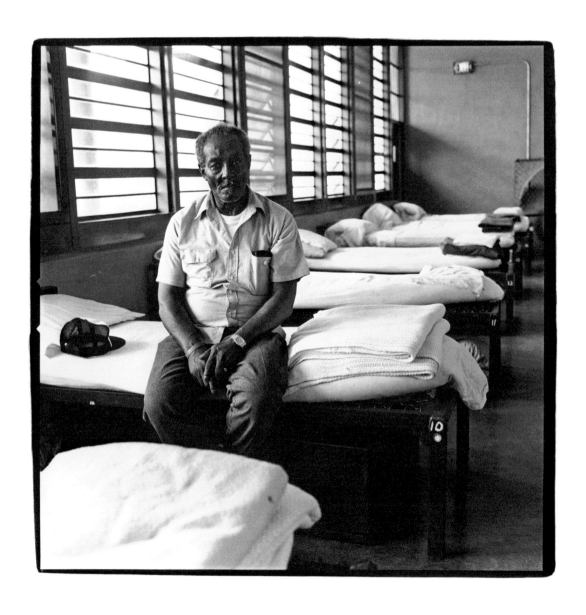

Moreese Bickham
PRISONER
LOUISIANA STATE PENITENTIARY, ANGOLA, LOUISIANA

I met Moreese Bickham in February 1990, when I spent a week down at the Louisiana State Penitentiary in Angola, Louisiana, producing "Tossing Away the Keys," a half-hour radio feature about men serving life without the possibility of parole at the nation's largest prison.

Angola looks like no other prison. The sprawling twenty-eight-square-mile plantation (named for the birthplace of the slaves who were once forced to work the land) is hemmed in by the Mississippi River on three sides and snake-infested hills on the fourth. Five thousand inmates are housed in six fenced-in prison camps, each surrounded by loops of razor wire and an army of security personnel. There is even a small town inside the penitentiary for the security staff (fifteen hundred strong), complete with a fire department, post office, and supermarket. Stepping into Angola has the feel of walking onto the set of an epic movie—long lines of black prisoners, shovels over their shoulders, marching in straight lines along the levees of the Mississippi, burly guards on horseback with shotguns resting across their laps trailing close behind.

Almost all of the lifers I had chosen to profile in "Tossing Away the Keys" had been caught up in extremely unlucky predicaments. At the time that each of them was initially sentenced for their crimes, "life" in Louisiana meant a maximum of ten years and six months behind bars. But just as their final year at Angola was approaching, Louisiana changed its life sentence statute to mean exactly that: no way out barring a pardon by the governor. Suddenly, these men were faced with the prospect of dying in prison.

Monroe Green, Joe White, Donald Buffet, Henry Patterson, and Moreese Bickham are among the longest of the long-termers incarcerated in the nation. All African-Americans, all convicted before the civil rights movement. They sat with me for hours in a bare office at Angola's main prison complex, describing the ordeal of growing old inside a maximum-security penitentiary. "I find technology amazing," Henry Patterson said. "I don't know for sure, but I hear they got 'superhighways' now—where you bypass the cities. I never rode on no superhighway. I wouldn't know what to do if I got on one. They say you got lanes that say 'fast' and 'slow.' And if you look at all these things you say, 'Boy, this is amazing!' Because I can only relate to what I came out of in '61, and when I came in here in '61 the restaurants were segregated. When I caught the bus, I caught the back of the bus. You look at the changes, and you wonder 'is it real?' "

"If you were buried alive, that's what it would be like," Joe White explained. "Except for the television, we wouldn't know there's a world out there. When we come here everything stops. It's as if you're in spirit and everything around you is alive, and you can't do anything but look. You can see but you can't touch."

For me, the most powerful testimonial came from Moreese Bickham. Unlike the other prisoners featured in the documentary, Bickham was serving a life term as the result of a commuted death sentence. Bickham was soft-spoken and gentle, an ordained minister of the Methodist Church. For the past several years, he had spent his days tending to a small rosebush patch near one of Angola's cafeterias. "I know it sound funny," he told me, clipping stems, "but these is my company-keepers. These bushes have come to be close, close—very close to me. If you don't see after them, they'll just die. That's the way some people do in prison. But me, I got a life to live, in here or out. Make the best you can out of a bad situation—that's what I've been doing all my life." What follows is an edited transcript of two long interviews with Bickham at the penitentiary.

———————————

My name is Moreese Bickham. My prison number is 75251, and I am seventy-two years old. I been in prison ever since 1958—goin' on thirty-two years. That's right. I was born in Mississippi, a place called Tylertown, and I lived there on the farm until I was twenty. I left, went to Louisiana, and then went into the service. I served in the navy, South Pacific, and got an honorable discharge in '46. When I come back, I went to Mississippi until '52, and then moved to Louisiana. A small town called Mandeville. Worked as a contractor, a carpenter. Never did have any trouble, except I spent two nights in jail once for drunk driving. But I was a black man living in a white neighborhood, and some people didn't like that too good.

My crime is murder of two white deputies in Mandeville. It was July the 12th, 1958. I was in a dance hall with my common-law wife. A little argument started, and she hit me over the head with a bottle. Well, the deputy come, and took her. Natural, I followed him on out, and when he put her in the car, I tried to get in. I said, "You want to arrest me, arrest me. Wherever you take her, take me." He said, "You get in the car, you so-and-so, I'll kill you." I said, "You will?" He said, "Yeah," and went and unbuckled his gun. I said "Well, you'll have to shoot me in the back," and started walking off. He said, "I'll get you." And I said, "When?" He said, "Tonight." When my wife went to get out of the car he said, "No, stay in there!"

I don't know when he got the other deputy or what happened, but anyway I had to walk about five blocks or six to my uncle's, 'cause my gun was there.

When I come home, I didn't see anybody. But when I stepped out of the house a little later to put the gun back at my uncle's, there they were. They came at me, an' one said, "He got a gun." An' the other say, "He oughta have one." An' I say, "It ain't loaded." And I put my hands up. He say, "It oughta be," and he shot me in the chest. I fell on my gun and loaded it. When he walked up to finish me off, I shot him. The other one, he run an' grabbed *his* shotgun and pulled it around, and I shot *him*. They both got killed.

That's the way it happen, and the people that were livin' in the place next door know that's the way it happen. *Everybody* know that's the way it happen. But the deputies were Klan Dragons, you know, and the Klan had the upper hand. At the trial, the Klan made sure that wouldn't nobody testify in my behalf, because they said if they did they was gonna burn up their houses and shoot 'em when they come out. Everybody was scared—even my father-in-law and my mother-in-law! So I didn't have anybody to testify in my behalf in my trial. I heard later that both of 'em had killed before. One had killed two men, the other one had killed four. This man—he was a deputy sheriff—told me I was supposed to be one of them's third one.

I lived with this thirty-some years, and the more I think about it, the more I can't understand how I got into this. Just one a' them things I don't understand. If I knew what was going to happen, I could have avoided it. And when I get to talkin' about it, and my mind goes back to that night, it was just a nightmare! Oh boy. It makes me feel like it might have been better if I got killed that night than to go through all I've been through. Man, man, man.

After the shoot-out, I was sentenced to death. I stayed in the death cell from the day I got locked up until '73—fourteen years and ten months on death row. I had a six-by-eight cell, and it come to be my home, and the fellows around me come to be my family. On death row, mens get closer than brothers, because on Monday to Friday you be expecting those death warrants to come at any time— you looking for someone to bring an envelope that say, "You go such-and-such a day." Then Friday evening to Monday morning we had a break—nobody would sign 'em on Saturday and Sunday. I had seven stays of execution—they set a date on me for four months straight, so I know what it's about. The closest I come was about fourteen hours away, from nine in the morning to twelve at night. Everyone in there swore they were gonna execute me, but by the help of good God, I ain't gone yet.

I fell off from death row in '73 when they abolished it—said it was unconsti-tutional. I got it commuted to life sentence, and I been out here on the farm with the population ever since. Right now I'm the oldest convict in this place. I've seen them go and come. There's men come in here with fifty years and have went out and come back again with ten *more* years, and now they going out *again*—all since I been here.

It's really a different world in here. You don't have any privilege of you own. None. They tell you what to wear, when to go, what to eat, when to lay down, when to get up, what side to walk on, when to speak. It take a grown person an' make a baby out of him. He gets dependent on it, you understand? You might say, "Well, I wanna go fishing." You can't go. You might say, "I wanna go visit somebody." You can't go. You might say, "Well, I'd like to call somebody, its ten o'clock at night." You can't call. That makes a man a vegetable. I can be sittin' there lookin' at TV, and I can hear a whistle blow on the TV, and think the man walked in the door and say, "It's count!" And I just get up and go on to the bed. After so long a time, it'll work on your mind.

Since I been locked up, I lost all my family mostly. I can see losing my mother and father, but all my brothers and sisters? All my aunts and uncles? The judge is dead, the DA's dead. Everybody's passed on but me. And when I look at it, I say, "Lord, why am I still here?" It makes you wonder. But if you look back at what happened to people in olden time and what they did to them, you see you got something to look forward to. They ain't thrown none of us in the lion's den or anything like that, at least.

In 1984, the pardon recommended my time be cut to forty years. It stayed on the governor's desk—that was Governor Edwards—his whole term and he didn't sign it. It was there when Governor Roemer come in, and he let it stay there for six more months, and then sent it back to me and said, "Try again in six months." Well, I went up in six months, and the pardon board recommended I get my sentence cut to time served and a full pardon. That stayed on his desk for five months, and then he sent it back—"*denied*." He didn't give no reason, and the pardon board said far as they concerned, case closed. But I know that as long as there's life, there's hope.

Now, a lot of people wonder how I make it. Youngster comes in here nineteen years old, and the judge give him ninety-nine years—throw him down that walk down there. And he adjusts hisself to what's going on and forget about the time they give him. He meets me and say, "How long you been here?" I say, "For thirty-one years." He says, "Huh?" I said, "Yeah." He say, "Well, man, if they won't let you out, ain't no chance for me." That makes a man mentally give up on life and makes 'em violent: suicide, murder—anything! I had one fellow say to me, I believe it was Valentine's Day, he said, "Man, if they turned me down as many times as they turned you down, I'd just go ahead and get it over with." I said, "Like what?" He said, "I'd make somebody kill me." I said, "Well, that's talk. That's easy to do. You'll get strong, and you'll learn to be a good fighter." I tell all these young fellas, "Maybe your case is different than mine, and you'll get out." Give 'em a little hope, you know. See, hope does something for a man—it makes him hang on to what little he got to get more. But if he lose that, there's nothin' to hang on to.

Point Lookout, we call it Boot Hill, is a place out there where they bury the dead at Angola. I worked out there taking care of the grounds for two years and four months, and the only two people that visited that cemetery was one old lady and an old man. I went to a friend of mine's funeral there in '84. His name was James Chrip—he used to be in the same dorm as me before he took sick and went to the hospital, and we were very close. I stood over his grave and read the twenty-third Psalm, and I had some tall thinking. The next year I paid for me a burial, to be buried in the cemetery alongside my mamma. Won't be buried at Point Lookout. See, if you buried out there you really forgotten. Nobody come out to visit, nobody even *passes by* Boot Hill. Old-timers think about that a right good deal, but they don't like to talk about it much, because they 'fraid they might end up out there.

My first night on death row I asked the Lord to show me was I gonna get out or not, and He said, "Don't worry, everything gonna be allright." That night I dreamed that I was out on a high mountain out West, looking at pretty cattle and green grass and water running. Momma was on one side and my sister was on the other and my grandma was in the midst. I looked around and said, "What you doin' here, Grandma?" She said, "I been with you ever since that night you got in this trouble." That's when I realized that God had sent a spirit to lead me through all this, and that I was gonna get out. See, we can't hurry the Lord—He got his own set time to do what He gonna do. I might be too old to walk, or might not be worth anything, but I'm goin' to get outta this. I been lookin' forward to that day for a long time. I believe its gonna come. I hope so.

In the years following the broadcast of "Tossing Away the Keys," several of the prisoners profiled in the documentary were pardoned and released. Moreese Bickham was not among them. Each time Bickham appeared before the pardon board, his appeal was strongly protested by the Mandeville Police Department. "We will do anything we can to keep him in prison," the town's chief of police said in a news-paper interview. "He has no business on the street after killing two police officers from ambush. Feelings are still hot in Mandeville over the murder."

After the broadcast of the documentary I kept in touch with Bickham through occasional cards and letters, but didn't delve more deeply into his case. It wasn't until I sat down to write this book in the summer of 1994 that I realized the mistake I had made.

As I began to research Bickham's story—no one had touched the trial materials in decades—I found Bickham's 1990 version of the crime to be identical to his confession of thirty-five years ago. The trial transcript is an eerie read. The prosecution's case against Bickham only seems to bolster his claims of self-defense. It seems that in pre-civil-rights Louisiana, self-defense was not an acceptable claim for a black man accused of killing two white law enforcement officers.

For the next eight months my friend Michael Alcamo, an attorney in New York, lobbied tirelessly on behalf of Moreese Bickham. After learning that Bickham's health was faltering, we orchestrated a small media blitz on his behalf. We asked people to contact Louisiana Governor Edwin Edwards's office and urge him to commute Bickham's sentence. The governor received thousands of letters and phone calls.

We were hoping Governor Edwards would sign Mr. Bickham's commutation papers over the holidays. Christmas came and went. We pressed on. In February 1995, we received devastating news: a highly placed political insider in Louisiana, whom Michael had persuaded to take an interest in Mr. Bickham's case, got a look at the file on the governor's desk. While the support letters were there, so were dozens of letters of opposition. Apparently the Mandeville Police Department and local politicians had redoubled their efforts to ensure that Bickham would remian behind bars for the rest of his life. This attorney told Michael it was all over. He'd never seen anyone with that kind of law enforcement opposition have his commutation signed.

Michael began making plans to shift strategy, bringing Bickham's case back to court on a habeas corpus petition challenging the conviction on the grounds that he hadn't received a fair trial. Freedom for Bickham seemed more elusive than ever.

Then, on the afternoon of March 13, 1995, I got an urgent message from Michael. I called him back. He was in shock. For some reason Governor Edwards had decided to sign Bickham's commutation, making him eligible for immediate parole. We got on the phone to his family. It was pandemonium. Screams. Tears.

One of his granddaughters, Selena Garrett, told us, "I feel like my grandfather's been raised from the dead." We all understood that we were witnessing a miracle.

Mr. Bickham is scheduled to be released from Angola on January 10th, 1996. He plans to move out to Oakland, California, to live with his wife, daughter, five grandchildren, and fourteen great-grandchildren. ■

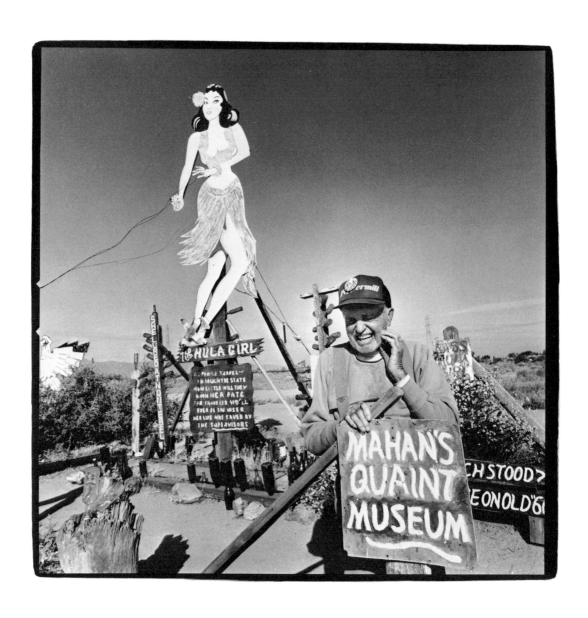

Miles Mahan
CREATOR, HULA VILLE
VICTORVILLE, CALIFORNIA

I found Miles Mahan and his Hula Ville Museum along Highway 15 near Victorville, California, at the edge of the Mojave Desert about one hundred miles northeast of Los Angeles, in June 1993. When I drove up, Miles was sitting on a junked couch underneath a Joshua tree, watching the traffic zip by. Beside him, Hula Ville: the dusty museum he's built up around a wooden cutout of a hula girl salvaged from a Hawaiian restaurant nearly forty years ago.

ISAY: *Excuse me, are you Miles?*

MILES: You're back again?

We never met before.

Well of all things! What are you doing here?

I'm doing a radio story about you.

You are?

If you don't mind

Not at all! That's a big laugh! Ha, ha, ha!

This is quite some place you have here.

Well, I built it myself. Built it from scratch. Found the hula girl in '55, you know. It was down on the side of the road. Put it up here. I wouldn't have a chance in the world if it wasn't for the hula girl. If it wasn't for this dame, there wouldn't be nothing here. Wouldn't be a thing! Let me tell you how I picked this spot. I was out with the carnival. Worked the carnival for *years*, guessing weights. I was pretty good at it. Anyway, one time they had this little carnival out here, and I met a fella who was trying to sell some real estate. He told me about a piece of land along the freeway here, and said it was for sale. I had a little money and I bought it. Now it's an attraction!

Can you give me a tour?

You bet I can. We'll go over here. . . . Now that right there's for the kids. They get on and ride it just like a horse.

But Miles, it's just a tree stump.

It is! I made a little seat for the kids, and get on it and ride. It don't buck much, but kids like to get into everything, you know. Come around this way. I don't want you to fall down. Now this platform here, I call it my Dance Pavilion. I do my dances on there. I used to teach dancing in Las Vegas. I taught that "slicker waltz." You know what a slicker is? I'll show you. You'll get the drift of it. This is how I did it. What I did was I slickered back and forth. This is the slicker waltz. [Begins to dance]

Careful, Miles, careful.

Hah! You thought I was going to fall?

You were going to fall.

Well, maybe I was. Ha ha ha. I damn near slid out from under me!

Miles, can I ask how old you are?

Well . . . I'm not dead! [Laughs] You want to find out how old I am, huh? I was born in 1896—just turned ninety-six a couple of days ago. Here's my ID card. My girlfriend is forty-two. She used to dance, too. Now you follow me. . . . I have a little golf course here. Miniature, you know. I had some players, but that was a long time ago. . . . Now this is hole number one—here's where you tee off.

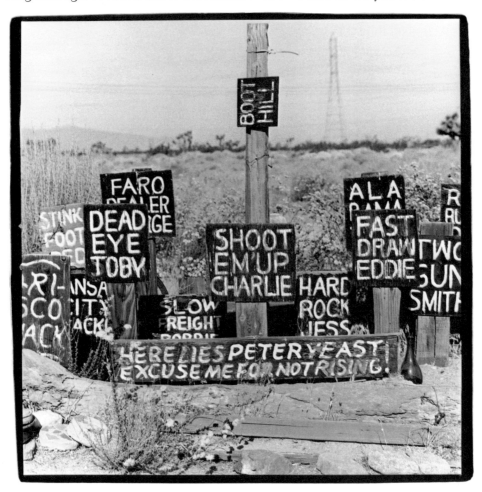

I don't quite see how this is a golf course—

Well, they have 'em now, miniature golf course. They have 'em all over!

But there are no—

They have grass now too, but I don't have the grass.

But Miles, there are no holes!

No, they like it this way! They don't have to stoop down, wear themselves out—they just kick it, and go tee off at the next one. It's more fun! You see that? Hole number six! I give that to God. He can have that.

Is it a shrine?

Yes. It's called "The Resurrection of Jesus."

You don't find that on every golf course.

[Laughing] No, you don't. And you don't find me either! ■

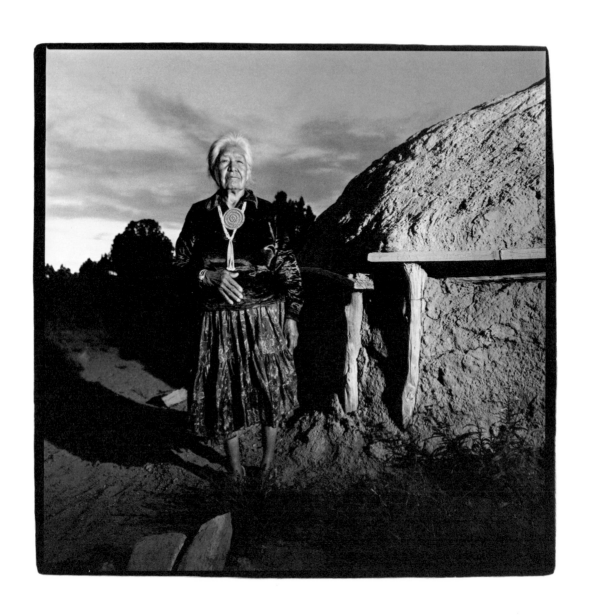

Roberta Blackgoat
Navajo Activist
Big Mountain, Arizona

From the nearest stretch of blacktop, it's a treacherous thirty-mile drive over a winding, deeply rutted dirt path to Roberta Blackgoat's home. "Hippity hop" is the understated term she uses to describe the brutal drive. "People don't come very often because it's so hard to get here!" The trek takes several hours. Don't try to find her without a guide.

Roberta Blackgoat lives far from electricity and running water in a small encampment of three ramshackle houses. Two of them are inhabited by families. Roberta, who was widowed thirty years ago, lives alone. "There is where I was born," she tells me, pointing to a spot in the sloping prairie where her parents' house once stood. "At least ten generations live in this land from my family. My five grandmothers are buried right here."

Roberta Blackgoat, great-grandmother and sheepherder, is an unlikely leader for a movement which has been resisting the government-mandated relocation of thousands of Navajo sheepherders from land they've lived and worked on for generations, the largest civilian relocation effort since the internment of Japanese-Americans during World War II. Over the course of the three-decade dispute, Roberta has protested tirelessly. She's been harassed and arrested. The messy, tragic, and complicated standoff known as Big Mountain remains far from resolved.

The saga began more than a century ago, in 1882, when President Chester A. Arthur signed an executive order designating the official boundaries of the Hopi Nation in north-central Arizona. The Hopis were deeded a 250-million acre rectangle of land around the three mesas on which they have lived for a millennium, surrounded on all sides by the much larger Navajo Nation. Unfortunately, the Bureau of Indian Affairs agent who drew these boundaries didn't do so as carefully as he might have. A good many Navajos were living on land which was now delineated Hopi, and a few Hopis were living on Navajo land.

Border squabbles between the two nations began almost immediately, but didn't come to a head until the early 1970s, when energy companies interested in the coal, oil, and uranium deposits on these reservations put pressure on the Interior Department to determine exactly which tribe owned what land. In 1974, Congress passed a law mandating that all of the disputed land be split down the middle, and authorized the relocation of all Native Americans who happened to fall on the wrong side of this divide. Almost all of the Indians affected were Navajo sheepherders (about ten thousand, versus the hundred or so Hopis who found themselves on Navajo land). Despite testimony from anthropologists that the move would wreak havoc on the men and women who'd lived there, the bill was pushed through the Senate by Arizona's Barry Goldwater (who detested then Navajo leader Peter MacDonald).

"At that time, I didn't realize what's going to happen," Roberta Blackgoat remembers. "I just make a lot of jokes. I say, 'I know they want the land for the mining. Why don't we just spread our wings and let them take out whatever they need? Then we can set back down again after they're gone.' That's what I said. I couldn't have thought that they meant for us to move away. Later on they told us that we had to look for where our new home is going to be set up. I said, 'No way. I'm not gonna move! All of our great-great-ancestors are buried here. Their spirits are still here. This is our sacred ground. Our altar is here, our songs and our prayers. We can't leave!' "

Roberta's resolve was only strengthened by what she saw happening around her once the relocations got under way. Typically, Navajo men and women were moved to homes in border towns. Ill prepared to navigate the Anglo-based economic system and unable to find work, the sheepherders found themselves faced with mounting bills and taxes. Loan sharks stepped in, offering to lend the Navajos money at exorbitant interest rates. Many of the Navajos took the offers, unaware that they were putting their homes up as collateral. By the third year of the relocation program, fully a third of the Navajos were homeless.

Whether or not they lost their homes, though, the move proved disastrous for Navajos involved in the relocation, particularly the older ones. "They get lonely.

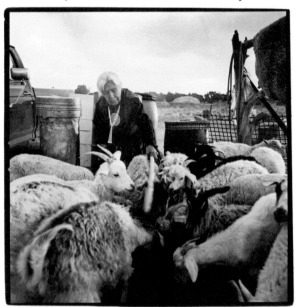

Lonely for the land," Roberta Blackgoat explains. "They get lonely for the songs and the prayers they have left back here. They go without their own food—like the mutton and the cornbread. They get sick. They are in tears. Most of the elders lost their lives out there. It doesn't take so long. That's why I said: 'If you transplant me elsewhere I will not grow, I'll just die.' "

It wasn't long after the relocation program began that Roberta Blackgoat, along with a few other elderly Navajo women, emerged as the matriarchs of the Big Mountain resistance movement. "When the policeman comes around with guns, if the men are in front, then they are liable to start using the gun. So that's why the women has to face first," explains Blackgoat, who, along with Katherine Smith, Pauline Whitesinger, and Alice Benally, all grandmothers in their sixties and seventies, took the lead in the fight to remain on their land. They picketed. They took down fences aimed at squeezing them off grazing ground. They ignored the laws mandating them to reduce their livestock. They constructed hogans despite a ban on new buildings. In the past several decades they have been arrested countless times. They have slept in jail cells. They have used bats and guns and fists to keep officials off the land they live on. And they remain resolved to keep fighting.

Despite coming close to mediated settlements several times, the Big Mountain standoff continues. Several thousand Navajo herders remain on the ground they believe to be their own. "I'm looking forward for my children and grandchildren and more to come," Roberta says. "Where are they going to be raised and learn how to use the land if there's no land for them to live on? I must stand here straight," she says, looking down at her feet. "I can't point my toes the other way, and make zigzag. I must stand right here and look forward. That's how I am." ■

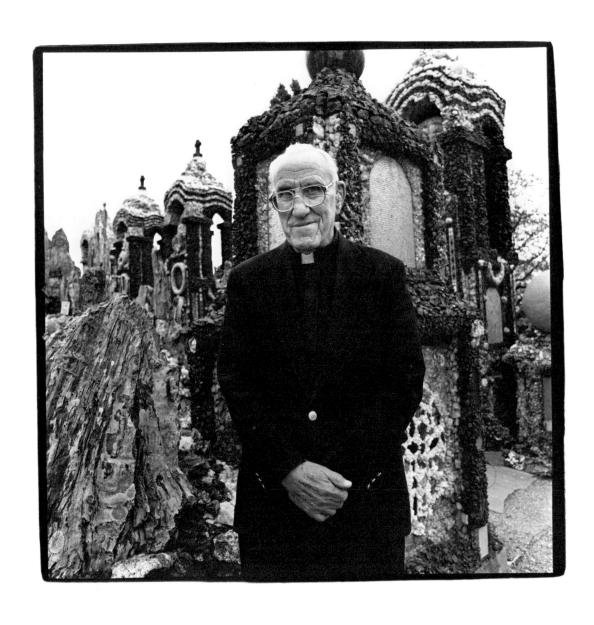

Father Louis H. Greving
BUILDER, GROTTO OF THE REDEMPTION
WEST BEND, IOWA

It's a startling sight, rising up from the sprawling cornfields of north-central Iowa, a bizarre organic structure that looks like a cross between a castle and a coral reef. The Grotto of the Redemption consists of eight caves connected to one another by stone paths and winding stairways. The entire structure has been covered with millions of tiny shards of stone and shell pressed into concrete and arranged into intricate patterns and pictures depicting scenes from the life of Jesus Christ.

The building of the Grotto of the Redemption was begun in 1912 by a priest named Paul Dobberstein, who worked tirelessly on the structure until his death in 1954. After that, construction was taken up by a priest named Louis Greving. To this day, if you visit West Bend, you're likely to find Father Greving carefully fitting pieces of stone into cement.

Father Louis Greving is an intense man. When talking about the Grotto, his voice rises and falls dramatically, quivering with emotion. At the end of sentences he freezes, his head tilted thoughtfully, his mouth fixed in a beatific smile.

I interviewed Father Greving on a Sunday afternoon in August 1992 inside one of the Grotto's eight caves, the Grotto of the Blessed Trinity. His voice echoed as he spoke. Religious music wafted from small speakers in the background.

This is the original grotto. The acoustics are positively beautiful—just listen to the reverberations. . . . WOW! [echoes] This is my favorite grotto. Why is it my favorite grotto? It represents the best of what Father Dobberstein, the builder, had in mind. Look up at the dome. Look closely and you see the stars, forty or fifty stars in the little dome. And you see the twenty angels adoring God? That represents heaven. This grotto represents such devotion and such careful artistic workmanship. It's a fulfillment of a promise.

This is what happened. Father Dobberstein came from Germany in 1890. He studied for the priesthood in Milwaukee, Wisconsin. About two weeks previous to his ordination, he became sick and went into the hospital. He begged his doctor to allow him to get out of his hospital bed to be ordained with his class. The doctor very hesitatingly said, "Okay, but right back to the hospital after the ordination!" Well, he was ordained a priest, and went back to the hospital. It turned out he had *double pneumonia*. That was almost quits for anybody—this was 1897. But he made a promise to our Blessed Mother: for the grace of health, sometime in his lifetime he would build a shrine in her honor.

He was sent here in 1898, and this is the grotto he had envisioned in fulfillment of that promise. He wanted to portray the life of Christ in stone, to express the whole story of the fall of man and his redemption through the way of the cross in nine different grottos. In 1900 he started picking up rocks and stockpiling them, and in 1912 he started building.

That man knew what he wanted to do. He was a little man, but he was determined. I never spent any time in my life with a man who was so taken up with his work as he was. He'd come on in the evening sometimes and his fingers would be bleeding from just putting these rocks into cement, and I'd say to him, "Well, Father, you'd better lay off and let these fingers heal up." And he'd say, "Ahh, but Father, there isn't any redemption without a little bit of blood." [Whispers] Wow! What do you say to something like that? The guy was not a phony!"

I was sent to assist Father Dobberstein after my ordination in 1946. We would have grotto for breakfast, we would have it again for lunch, and again in the evening. So this is the way I learned it. I knew the man. I saw his motivation. I saw his work. I saw his prayer. I saw his pain. I saw his determination. Day after day, night after night. Two o'clock in the morning I'd hear the clip of the hammer—winter and summer, and he was setting rocks into cement. Day after day, week after week. This is a monument to perseverance! He worked until two weeks before he died. What did he die of? Just hard work—he suffered a stroke. He would have been eighty-one years of age in a couple of months.

I worked with him for eight years as his assistant, so when Father died, the bishop left me here to continue the construction of the Grotto, to carry out Father Dobberstein's plan. When I started, the Grotto of Bethlehem and the Grotto of Nazareth were not built yet. Today there are eight grottos. He envisioned nine. The Pentecostal Experience Grotto, we're still working on that. I hope to have that finished before I reach seventy-five. I hope so, but you know, if I don't, somebody else will. There's another man who is being groomed to take my place.

It's hard work to get on out there on a hot day when it's ninety degrees, and you start sticking rocks into cement. Sometimes I get so enthusiastic about it that I just stay at it as if I was twenty-five years, and then the old creaky bones, you see, they pay for it. Father Dobberstein used to say, "I only met one man that is as determined as I am," he said, "and that's you!"

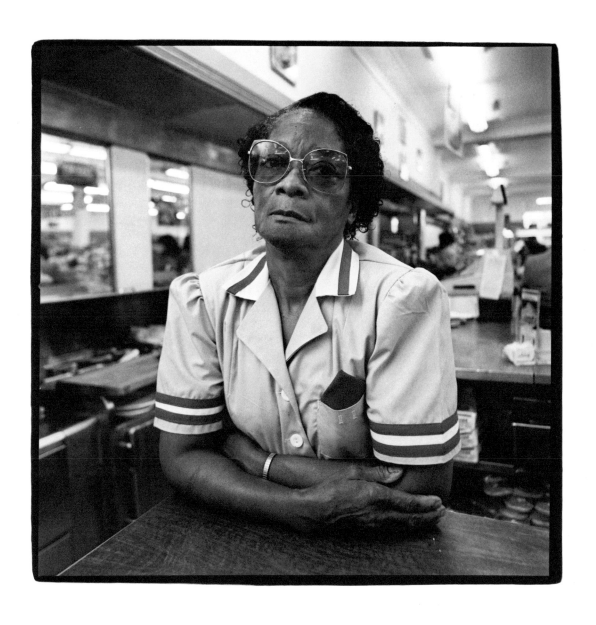

Geneva Tisdale
COOK, WOOLWORTH'S LUNCH COUNTER
GREENSBORO, NORTH CAROLINA

When Harvey and I read that the Woolworth's in Greensboro was closing down, we called the store to find out if there was anyone still serving food who'd worked at the lunch counter since the sit-in movement was born there in 1960. The manager called Geneva Tisdale to the phone. She told us that she had no time to talk—she was too busy with customers—but to please call her at home. We spoke with her that evening. She said she'd been working behind the counter for forty-two years, and was indeed present for the historic sit-ins. We called Woolworth's corporate headquarters in New York to get permission to tape and photograph Ms. Tisdale. They told us not to bother—they weren't allowing any media in the store. We flew down anyway, and after a bit of prodding, the store's manager decided to give Harvey five minutes to shoot a portrait at the counter. I interviewed Ms. Tisdale that evening, after she finished work.

My first name is Geneva. "Jane" is what they call me at work. See, I worked for a lady before I started working at Woolworth's, and she had two little girls that couldn't pronounce my name. They could say "Jane," so the lady said, "Let's call her Jane." So most of my working people think Jane's my real name. I'm sixty-one, and I been working at Woolworth's forty-two years now.

Started off in '51 as a fountain girl—made all the sundaes, milk shakes, banana splits, and things like that. Miss Rachel Holt was the manager at the time, and she would put you anywhere that she needed you. If the steam-table girl quit, she put me on the steam table. If the sandwich-board girl quit, she put me on the sandwich board. If she needed a glass washer, I washed glasses. Well, I got tired of her moving me around. They couldn't keep nobody on the sandwich board, so I told her one day, "From now on, that's going to be my job!" And I've been on it ever since. I've had people come in and ask, "How did you stay here so long?" And I have to think about how long it's been. When you busy you don't stop to think about it. I put myself in my work. Always have.

I think back how everything was made from scratch when I first started working here. The potatoes you had to peel the old-timey way. The pies were all made from scratch. All the vegetables was fresh vegetables. Everything. It wasn't no "instant this" and "instant that." The kitchen was full of people at that time, and that was a lot of hard work! Long hours.

They didn't have black waitresses. The blacks was the ones preparing the food, but the waitressess were all white. A lot of people at the counter did not know who was preparing that food. All the white people was sitting and enjoying the food, and a lot of time you would hear them saying . . . things. I would listen and say to myself, "You don't know that the same one you talking about is the one that's preparing your food!" It made you feel funny—I'm not good enough to sit at the counter with then, but I'm good enough to fix their food.

I remember the first day when the boys came in and sit down. The four students. At the time I was working the back steam table. I remember every time somebody would pass by 'em, they would ask if they could be served: they asked for a piece of pie and a cup of coffee. And everybody passed by 'em and just told 'em that they couldn't serve 'em. At first I thought they was just being funny. But then it made me kind of nervous, because I was carrying my last child, so I went on to the back and I stayed back there.

Well, they kept coming back. More and more people. Soon they took every seat in the store. I remember that good. I mean it was surrounded. Surrounded! They took the whole lunch counter, and they just sit there with books, studying. Couldn't serve anybody, so the store closed down for a period of time to decide what they were going to do.

When they reopened, Miss Holt called us out and told us how they were going to open the lunch counter to everybody. She said, "I want three of my girls to be served first when it reopens." And I was one. Anetha Jones was one—she deceased now. And Susie Kimber. Miss Holt told us, "When you come in tomorow, bring you some clothes like you gonna be customers." So we got to work, and she came over and she said, "Now you all go upstairs, get dressed, and walk around in the store like you a customer shopping," she said, "then come on over to the counter." And she told us where to sit. She said, "Now if you don't want your pictures in the paper, order something that you can eat real quick, 'cause when the word gets out, the newspaper people will be in here." I ordered a egg salad sandwich, and I swallowed it! [Laughs] It took me about five minutes. When we finished she said, "Go back upstairs, change back into your uniform, come back down, and go to work, and let's see what happens." So we done that, and sure enough it wasn't long before the photographers and people start crowding in—and they didn't know it was us! We were the first! [Laughs] I want it to be known that it was Woolworth's employees was the first to be served.

I tell you, I never did sit at the counter after that. That was the only time. And I was hoping that one day I'd be able to retire and come back and sit and have lunch. Just sit at the counter and be served. That's what I was hoping for. When the manager told us last week that Woolworth's was gonna close, he said he thought around the 1st of January. So I thought, "At least I have three more months." Then he said the lunch counter was gonna close first. This coming Saturday would be the last day for the luncheonette. So that was a shock. Didn't give you time to think. The lunch counter will be missed. I will miss it.

Talking about the civil rights movement, I don't think things will ever get to the point of "equal rights" where it will be equal. A lot have changed, but in some ways it's still as it always have been, like I still get paid five-fifty an hour after all these years. And I feel sometimes if a white person had this job, that person would get paid more than me. Just because the color of their skin. ■

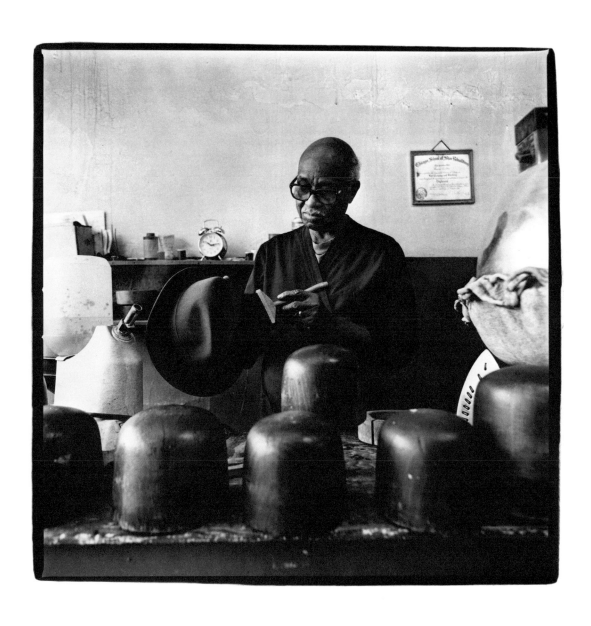

Harold C. Cotton
HAT BLOCKER
GREENSBORO, NORTH CAROLINA

Once in a while, serendipity played a role in finding stories. Such was the case with Bob's Hat Shop, a hat-blocking and shoeshine shop in Greensboro. After interviewing Geneva Tisdale about her career at Woolworth's, Harvey and I were driving around town looking for a place to spend the night. We passed an ancient storefront with a faded sign in the window: "Bob's Hatter's." Harvey insisted we pull over. I got out my tape recorder, Harvey got out his camera, and Harold Cotton took care of the rest.

The name of this place is Bob's Hat Shop. The person that opened it up, his name was Robert Taylor. He opened it in 1935, and I started working for him in 1937. I was in high school shining shoes on the street, and I had a cousin that worked in here. So I come in here one night, and I saw Mr. Taylor and in a joking way I said, "What about a job?" He said, "Can you shine shoes?" I said, "Yes, I can." So he got on that back seat and told me to shine his shoes. And when I finished shinin' his shoes, he said, "When you want to come to work?" And I said, "Right now!" So I been in and out of here since then—that was in 1937.

After that I went in the army. Then I went to hat blocking school in Chicago and come back here. I worked part-time at this store, contemplating opening up my own place. Well, the fella that owned this place, Mr. Taylor, he died in 1948, and there was another fella that bought it. But he got sick, so his sister run the place. One day we went to the hospital to visit him, and he told his sister, "If anything should happen to me, let Cotton have the shop." And I told him, "Don't worry 'bout that. Your main thing is gettin' well." Thirty days later, though, he did die. So his sister let me pick up the payments and says, "It's your shop." I been running it ever since. And a lot of people look up at the sign and see me in here and call me Bob. I answer to that. It doesn't bother me, 'cause when they get a chance to know me on an intimate basis they will start callin' me Cotton.

At the time that I got this shop, this time of day you couldn't hardly walk down here, so much traffic. They called this Hamburger Square, because on each corner they had a restaurant. One was named Jim's Lunch, which was a lot of people's favorite, then you had the Sunrise, which was on that corner over there, and then you had the California Lunch. Everybody had their particular place they liked to go. It was a very crowded area, but it was a blighted area too. Some of everything went on down here, some of everything that you can name.

You had the girls on the corner, and you had that hotel over there in particular. One fella shot a girl in that hotel, but she didn't die. It was his girlfriend, and he had to make time for it. They announced in the paper about two days before he would be getting out. So what she did, that same girl he shot, is she went and bought him a suit, a pair of shoes, shirt, tie, and a ring. And when he got out, that's what she put on him. And then we saw them walking up and down the street embracing each other. She's dead now, but he comes up on the corner every now and then.

So it's been a very interesting corner. Lot of things have happened up here. Fighting, drinking, making love—you name it they did it. That's what they did on this corner, outside this shop. And here we was doing our business. But it all went together. It all went together. [Laughs]

Now, gettin' back to the shop. . . . When I first started workin' here, a shoeshine was five cents—we talking almost fifty years or better since then. Now a shine costs two dollars. We also clean and block hats. See, a lot a people, when they take their hats off, they abuse them. When I was going to hat cleaning and blocking school I was taught how you really take a hat off, but I don't tell the customers that. That keeps us in business. You see, hats used to be mandatory thirty-five and forty-five years ago. If a person was a salesperson, that was the proper dress wear: a hat, a shirt, and a tie. But not anymore. This is just an assumption of mine, I don't have to be right, but President Kennedy, when he was elected President, he had a bushy head a' hair, and he didn't wear a hat. And it seemed to me during that particular period of time people stopped wearin' hats, and that just kind of caught on. But we still stay pretty busy. It's a seasonal thing.

First thing is we got a cleaning solvent in the back, and we put the hat in the cleaning solvent and we scrub it by hand. Then we let it drip awhile. Then after it drips we got a extractor back there we throw on it to get the rest of the cleaning fluid out. Then we put it in the window to dry. Then, when it's dry, we put it on the block—some people call it a mold—and we steam it to soften the felt. Then we press it flat with an iron. Then we put it right here on the spinner and we reshape it. You have to have almost a photostatic mind, 'cause you try to remember what each hat looked like when it comes in here. So from memory you put the shape back into it, press it, and that's it. So these is all hats waiting to be picked up. Some a' them hats been there long enough for me to sell or throw away. But I don't. You see, because I could probably reach down there right now and get one a' these hats and sell it to you. The moment you got out of sight, a guy could come in here an' say, "Cotton, you still got my hat?" I look down, and it would be the one I just sold you. [Laughs] So I don't sell 'em and I don't throw 'em away.

Now this is what I forgot to tell you about. You see this place, even though it's been owned by blacks ever since it been in business, at one time blacks could not sit on the shine stand. What they had to do was we had a big chair sitting in the back, and if blacks wanted to sit up on the stand they had to go to the back, and we would shine their shoes when we didn't have nothin' to do out here. That's the way it was at that particular time.

And then what happened was during the civil rights struggle and the Woolworth thing, they was demonstratin' downtown, and a black Marine happened to come in that door while they was demonstrating. We hadn't integrated then, and he said, "Can I get a shine?" I said, "Have a seat." So he got up on there, and I shined his shoes. So when he left out, the friend that I had working with me—he's dead now—I told him, "From now on," I said, "anybody that come in here can get up on the stand. I don't care whether they close us up or not."

Well, the fella that owned the property come in here on Saturday to collect the rent, and he saw all these people in here— I guess there was about three blacks on the stand, two whites, and the rest of the place was just full up. He said, "Mr. Cotton, when you get time, I'd like to see you outside." I went out and stood under that tree right there, and he said, "I see you've integrated the place." I said, "Most certainly have." And he said, "Are you having any problems with that?" And I said, "None so whatever." And he said, "If you're satisfied, I'm satisfied." And that's all he ever said. And from then on never did have one bit of trouble in here 'bout people sittin' next to one another. No trouble at all. ■

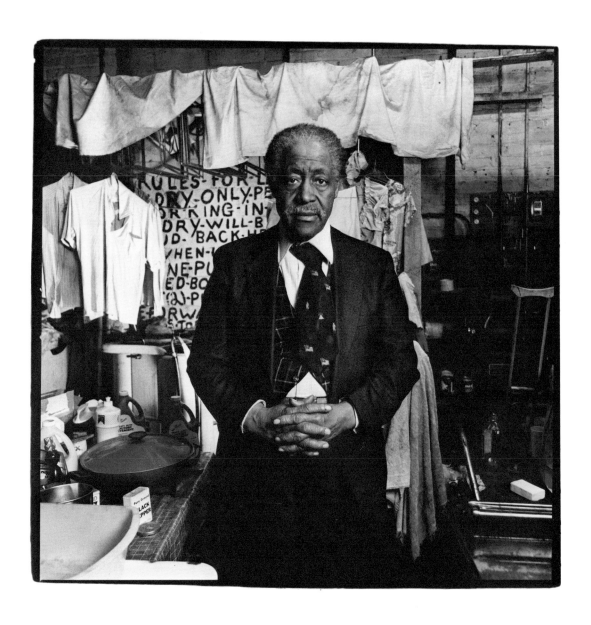

The Reverend "Prophet" William J. Blackmon

OVERSEER, REVIVAL CENTER TABERNACLE CHURCH
MILWAUKEE, WISCONSIN

The sign on the barbed-wire fence which surrounds the Revival Center Tabernacle Church reads: "Prophet 'tis in — blow horn." Honk, and Prophet Blackmon promptly emerges. "Very humbly," he'll explain, unlatching the padlocked gate, "God made me a prophet; I am a prophet of God. By the way, have you been having some little pressure headaches? Uh huh — God's taking care of that right now. Amen, amen. We thank God for that. Amen. . . ."

Prophet William J. Blackmon (he refers to himself as "God's Modern Apostle") inhabits a dilapidated brick warehouse in northwest Milwaukee, the inside of which nearly defies description. The building serves not only as Prophet Blackmon's church, but also as his shoe repair shop, laundromat, flea market, and home. Pipes from a series of makeshift stoves and heaters zigzag through the room, which is crammed with stacks of old mattresses, cobwebbed racks of used clothing, and a variety of other assorted junk.

The best time to visit Prophet Blackmon is on a Sunday morning, when the Revival Center Tabernacle Church holds its services. The congregation consists of three women and two men. Prophet Blackmon stands before them at a lectern, alternately prophesying, preaching, and breaking into song (at which time he heads to the back of the room to bang indiscriminately on the keys of a dilapidated piano).

The services go on for hours, which gives a visitor ample time to take in the scenery. On the walls, Prophet Blackmon has hung a series of crudely painted wooden signs. The messages are enigmatic, and read like verse:

> SHOES Str
> etched 75 ¢
> in shop pic
> up till 3:00

or:

> Help us to
> feed the
> hungry clothe th
> e naked
> order ou
> r magiz
> ines testim
> onies for Jesus

Indeed, these signs helped launch Prophet Blackmon on yet another career. Over the past several years Blackmon has emerged as one of the country's hottest folk artists, with his signs and paintings fetching thousands of dollars apiece.

This interview was conducted in the Prophet's art studio, a small space cordoned off from the rest of the warehouse by several racks of old overcoats. The studio consisted of a table, a chair, a few brushes in a pitcher of water, three cans of house paint, and a broken television set.

Way back I had a shoeshine stand in Chicago on the corner of Forty-third and Prairie. There was this Baptist Church, the Christian Hope Missionary Baptists Church, about a block from me. One day this young lady from the church says to me: "You got to come to my church." So I walked on up there with her. Now, during that time I used to suffer with gas pretty bad, after eating those pinto beans and so forth, so I'd take one Parke Davis pill before I ate, and one Parke Davis pill after. Well, we go inside this church, and the preacher's preachin' and says, "If you really believe in God you don't need no medicine!" So when I got outside the building I threw the pills away! I hadn't even told the people that I wanted to join the church yet! Do you know it was about three months later that I realized I was completely healed? No more gas! That was God himself.

After that I joined the church—they made me a junior deacon on trial—and strange things began to happen. I used to walk all over Chicago doing mission work. One day I went to this house. I knocked on the door and I said, "Anybody sick here?" And the lady said, "My daughter is. Come on in." Her daughter had a heart condition. She was bedridden. I said, "I'm gonna pray for her, and I believe God's going to heal her." Just like that. I laid my hands on her (during that time the sweat would just run off my hands when I laid my hands on a person—there was so much fire coming through my body), and then when I stepped back she took three long breaths and jumped up out of the bed. It scared me half to death, you know! [Laughs] I'm just a junior deacon on trial, you understand, but by faith I laid hands on her and she was healed.

After that, people would come to the church and tell the pastor that they was healed by me. The pastor would look at me funny, you know. And when my pastor would be preaching—all talking and waving all over—sometimes I'd get up and I'd say, "Pardon me." And he'd say, "What is it, brother Blackmon?" And one time I said, "I believe there's gonna be a storm in three days," Then I said, "I'm sorry I interrupted," and sat back down real quick. I felt bad, like I done the wrong thing. Three days later I was caught in the storm! It was an electrical storm, and the lightning came so close I could feel the heat. I'll never forget it! So that was the beginning, more or less, for the gift of prophecy.

I finally told the preacher that I wanted to preach. He didn't want me behind the pulpit because he thought I was going to take away his congregation. It was jealousy. He ordained his son and let him preach. So I got on the highway and threw a thumb up for a ride, and that was the beginning of my hitchhiking ministry.

I was a hitchhiking man of God for forty years or more. I didn't have money, but I just felt the drive of God to go and preach the gospel. So I learned to have faith. When you're hitchhiking, you eat when you can and you sleep when you can. I spent most my time in colored neighborhoods. I'd knock on the door and I'd let them know I was a minister. "Do you have anyone sick?'" And if they did I prayed for them. With most of them I could tell them what the trouble was right away, so they'd know God must be in the plan. Then it'd be getting late, suppertime, and they'd say, "Well, preacher, we gettin' ready for supper. Are you hungry?" And I'd say, "Well, I could eat something." A lot of times they made a mistake by telling me, "Make yourself at home." See, after you've been out on the highway for four or five hours trying to get a ride and somebody tell you to make yourself at home, well, that big plate of chicken is going to disappear! Then after I'm gone, they can say whatever they want about this old preacher: "See how much he ate?" I'm going down the highway saying [he shouts] "Praise the Lord" [laughs]—because I've got a full stomach. It's beautiful. That's when God becomes real to you!

I must tell you about my art. Now Sister Rosetta Farrow, who has this great gift of prophecy, one day it came to her mouth: "God's gonna make an artist out of you! You gonna be painting!" Maybe three years before I started, it came out of her mouth just like that! Well, back then I had my shoe repair shop at 300 West Juneau. One winter I made a whole lot of signs and hung them up all around the building telling about the shoe repair. I was doing all I could to drum up some business—I was closing on Friday and Saturday sometimes with no more than thirty dollars and I was feeding the people on the street with that money too!

On one particular Saturday I was at the shoe repair shop, and here comes this white lady, and she says, "Oh, how wonderful!'" I said, "What's that?" And she said, "Your signs!" And I said, "Signs?" She said, "Yes!" And she looked and said, "Would you sell this to me?" And I say, "Well. . . ." I thought she maybe she would give me five dollars and that would be allright, amen. Then she looks at me and says, "Will one hundred dollars do?" I was closing with twenty or thirty dollars, a week see—so it took me by surprise. And so that was the way it all started.

Being a man of God I'm gonna tell you that until I started selling my art I didn't have a place to stay. The street ministry, you see, is the roughest, so I was sleeping on a little mattress at 300 West Juneau. And that's where I started to paint. I would go into the alley and get the old wood that people had throwed away, and that's what I was painting on. I was turning out some historical work! And I used water paint—regular paint that you paint houses with. And it worked. It worked! Isn't that something?

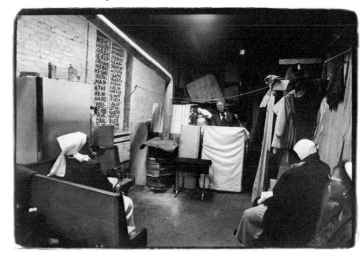

You have to have an inspiration. All artists will tell you that. So I meditate to God. I might sit here for an hour or two. I get the Bible. Finally I see a story about someone, and there's the inspiration! Like Daniel in the Lions' Den—I did that. The Escape from Moab—that was a very special piece, you know. And when I finish and I stand back and look at it I say, "Oh my." I'm amazed! And I know it's not me, I know its inspiration from God—so I end up giving God all the praise and all the glory.

And now the inspiration is really flowing. The prophecy that comes forth is that the art is going to be greater. Much greater! I'm believing now that people are going to begin to get healed just by *looking* at the art. To me it's coming just that great, because I can feel something unusual. I haven't heard yet that somebody has come through the gallery and looked at something and their headache left, or their stomachache—but I believe that it's going to be. And that's what's going to make it even greater! Right! Amen! God bless you! God bless you! ■

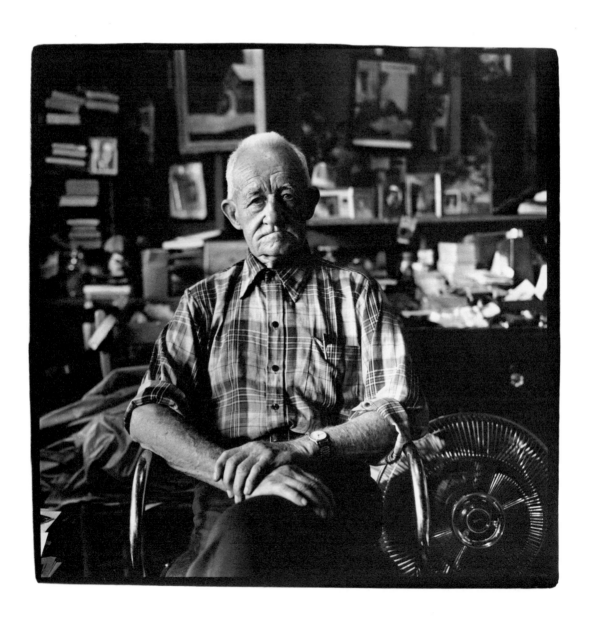

Tommie Bass
Folk Doctor
Leesburg, Alabama

Folk doctor A. L. "Tommie" Bass spends his days planted in a chair outside his home on the southern edge of the Appalachian hills, his hands folded on his lap, waiting patiently for customers. "We've been in the herb business ever since 1918," he explains (Tommie always refers to himself as "we"). "Never made a dime out of it, but we sure have seen people get better!"

Bass lives in a run-down shack with no running water at the foot of Lookout Mountain near Centre, Alabama. He supplements his meager income as an herb doctor by running a junk business from his front yard. I interviewed Tommie Bass in his home late one evening in November 1992.

Well sir, it's really a long story, sir. I was a little old poor boy back in nineteen and eighteen when we moved over on the side of Lookout Mountain. My daddy was a fur dealer—he bought all kinds of furs: possum, coon, mink, muskrat. All of the fur houses in the cities, they bought medical herbs. I could dig up these herbs and some of them would bring in ten cents a pound, some fifteen, and some twenty. I could ship a hundred pounds from Leesburg to St. Louis on a freight train for a dollar sixty-five cents. Well, if I had ten dollars' worth, by gosh it was all profit except that dollar sixty-five. After I got bigger—'course I just weighed sixty pounds when I was sixteen years old—the people around here started to hear about me, and they would want me to get this and that herb, and I'd go out and I'd go out and get it for them. A lot of times I'd stay in the woods all day long, getting herbs.

One of the first cures I had was a young fellow. This fellow comes to me—he's dead and gone now—and he said, "Hey, do you know what red shank is?" I said, "Well sure, fella. What are you going to do with it?" He said, "Well, Dr. Gramlin is doctoring my little girl, three years old, and he said she's got colitis and she's just got about three days to live." Of course, everybody thought that if Dr. Gramlin told you that you was gonna die, you just as well go ahead get in the grave, because you was gone. "Aunt Molly Kirby," he said—she was an herbist and a midwife that delivered more babies than all the doctors around here— "She calls you the 'herb boy.' She said for me to come and see you, and for you to dig the red root and make a tea. She said in three days the little girl would be eating anything she wanted." And this man, when he got excited he stuttered, he said, "I'll, I'll t-t-tell you wh-wh-what I'll do, I'll give you f-f-five dollars to get me enough to make me some tea." I said, "Man, you mean to tell me that you think I'd charge you five dollars to get something to cure your little girl?" He says,

"Dammit, I don't know!" Well, I went on down there and dug up the herbs. He made the tea and the little girl was eating anything she wanted in three days. And, oh boy, it just made me feel so good to think that she was back on the road again!

Later on, we had a man and his wife that lived over at Oak Grove, Alabama. They come over and say, "Tommie, we hear you know all about herbs." I said, "What's your trouble?" They said, "Our son has got sugar diabetes in the worst way. Do you know anything that will help him?" I said, "Now I'm not gonna tell you that it will cure him, but it will help him." I said, "Come down here in the pasture and I'll get you some queen of the meadow." And I dug them up a bunch of it. Well, they went on home, and about six months after that they come back and said, "Well, that beats anything we've ever seen! Our son don't have no diabetes—it just healed solid well!" And I said, "Well, I sure am so proud that it healed 'im." And by gosh he went in the army and was just fine. We didn't make any money out of it, but we was just so glad he was better, you see.

Coming on up many years after that, there was a woman and her daughter in a car wreck, and it just like to kill both of them. The little girl was twelve years old and it wrecked her kidneys to where she couldn't even go to school—she couldn't hold her water. Well, her daddy come here to tell me this, and I said to him, "Well, mister, that's a serious affair," I said, "but I think what we need to do is to give you daughter squaw vine tea. I've got enough to make about a half a gallon. You take it home, and make her drink a half a teacup full of it two or three times a day." Well by gosh in about two or three weeks she went back to school—kidneys getting better. And after she drank that all up, her father come back and said, "Well, Tommie, I actually believe if we had about another half a gallon it would cure her." And I went over in the woods and got enough of the squaw vine to make a half gallon of tea. Now she's a married woman and got a good family, you know—just cured her sound and well—wouldn't even ever know she had a kidney condition!

Now you take the common peach tree. If you want to sleep, just take a handful of peach tree leaves, put 'em in a teacup, run the hot water over 'em, let it set about ten minutes, and drink it. Boy, you better have your bed ready because you're going to get sleepy. And if you have the nerves, just shaking all over, drink a cup of the tea and you'll be as quiet as a baby. It's wonderful what it will do. And for morning sickness, expecting mothers can drink the tea at night, and in the morning no more morning sickness—just kills it graveyard dead! And then there's the magnolia tree for rheumatism and arthritis—just peel the bark, take a teacupful, and boil it in a quart of water for about twenty-five minutes and strain it. Keep it in the 'frigerator, and drink a swallow of it two or three times a day, and boy it just takes them pains away. And Queen Anne's lace—it takes the weight off you just like water. But bitter—boy, is she bitter! 'Course, here we got sage, which is the finest thing in the world for a hair tonic—just wash your hair in sage tea— it actually will make hair grow from a doorknob. [Laughs] And of course, down through the years the yellow poplar and the white for indigestion and for high blood pressure and heart trouble. They really do work! It's just nature, you know—natural.

We don't claim to be a doctor. Don't have no doctor's license, never did study it. I'm just an herbist. I studied how the herbs works on the human being, and how they've helped 'em. Over in the University of North Carolina there was a bunch of doctors there, and they knew that I was a hillbilly, and they was gonna have some fun out of me. They wanted to know how I diagnose cases, so I told

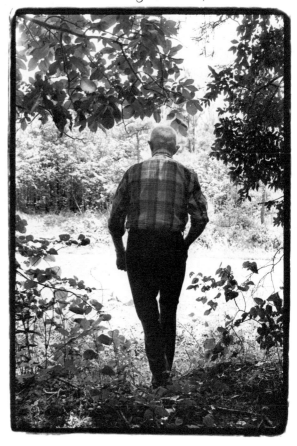

'em that I didn't diagnose no cases. I said, "Men, I'm not a doctor. Not even a son of a doctor. All I know is just what the herbs has done over the years. I've seen it actually happen. The drugs didn't do no good, and they took the herbs and they got back on the road again." And I said, "I don't tell anybody to take the herbs if they don't want to, but if they wish to, well, there's no harm in it—not a bit of harm in the world!" I been into it, you see, for around seventy-two years. If a fella' don't learn something in that time, he might just as well quit! ■

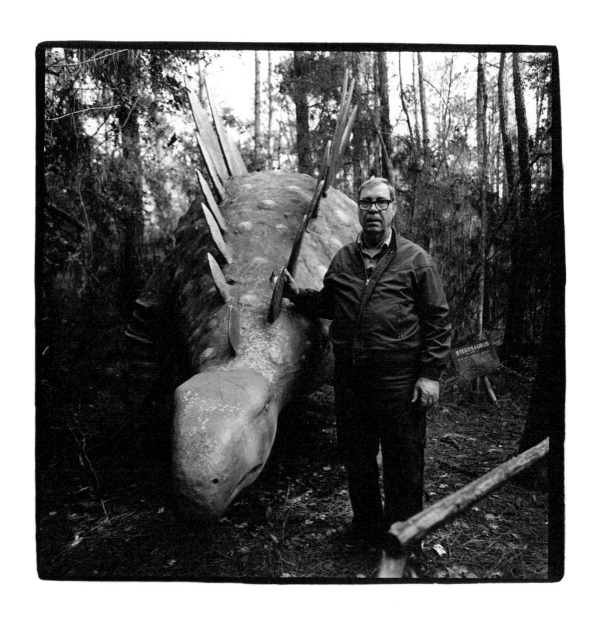

Donald Bean
PROPRIETOR, DINOSAUR GARDENS
MOSCOW, TEXAS

"I Thought I Saw a Dinosaur" reads the welcome sign to Moscow, Texas, an unincorporated hamlet ninety miles north of Houston. There isn't much more to this place. Indeed, the number of dinosaurs residing in Moscow rivals the town's population, all thanks to a retired carpenter named Donald Bean.

"I try to keep this as much as I can like it would have been back then, you know," Bean explains as we begin our tour through the roadside attraction. Canned dinosaur sound effects erupt from small speakers hidden in the trees. We round a corner and come upon the theme park's first dinosaur—Elasmosaurus, a twenty-foot-long flippered beast residing in a murky bog of water, surrounded by a ring of pond scum. "If you cleaned it out," Bean explained, "it wouldn't be a swamp."

All told, Donald Bean's roadside attraction consists of exactly eleven worn fiberglass dinosaurs laid out along a winding trail cut into the woods behind his home. Bean opened up Dinosaur Gardens in 1981—the culmination of a lifelong fascination with these prehistoric creatures. "I always liked dinosaurs. They're large, they're big, and they ruled the world for years. . . . Thousands of years. . . . Well, *millions* of years!" Donald Bean came up with the idea for the theme park in the late 1950s when he happened upon a similar roadside attraction in Oregon while vacationing with his wife, Yvonne. "Soon as I saw that I said, 'That's what I want to do!' So I did it."

It took Bean twenty years of planning and saving before he was finally ready to build his own theme park. "My wife wasn't too for the idea right off the jump go, because we spent our life savings on it." The park cost the Beans nearly $100,000 to build, and when Dinosaur Gardens opened it was met with just about the level of enthusiasm one might anticipate for a dinosaur theme park in the heart of Moscow,

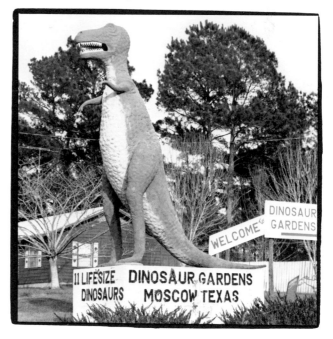

Texas. The masses did not seem to share Bean's fervor for creatures prehistoric. There were no lines at the ticket office. "It kind of disappointed me," Bean says, wiping a spider web from Struthiomimus's mouth. "I don't know how many people I thought would come, but I thought there'd be quite a few."

For twelve years now, business has been extremely slow at Dinosaur Gardens. There are two ways to look at the situation, though. There is a downside, to be sure: Bean's wife of forty-three years has had to come out of retirement and take a job at a nearby convenience store in order to help support her husband's dinosaur habit. But there's an upside, too. With visitors scarce, Donald Bean can spend all the time as he wants, alone in his theme park, pondering his dinosaurs. "A lot of times in the evenings or the mornings I just saunter down through here, and just go slow and look 'em over. And if you got a lot of imagination, you just feel like you're back in time, you know. . . . You can think what these things do when you're not here. Like this one," Bean explains, pointing at his Dimetrodon. "I think in my imagination he'd move slow and sluggish, unless something scared him or he was running for food—in that case he'd be real fast! And if you're walking down through here (unless you're a little kid), you know they're not gonna bother you, so you walk along and you can imagine all the *good* things about them. . . . It just brings you back to the time when they was here!" ▪

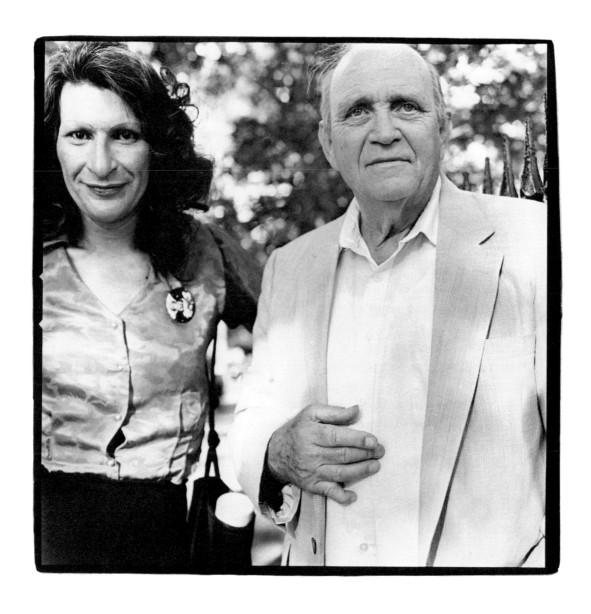

Sylvia (Ray) Rivera and
Deputy Inspector Seymour Pine
VETERANS OF THE STONEWALL RIOTS
NEW YORK CITY

On the night of June 27, 1969, a gay bar in Greenwich Village, the Stonewall Inn, was raided by the vice squad. It was nothing out of the ordinary—at the time, gay bars were routinely shut down by the police. Typically, patrons would quietly submit to any and all orders given and disperse peacefully, afraid their identities might be revealed to their families, friends, or employers. But this June night at the Stonewall Inn was different. The patrons of the bar, led by a small but determined group of drag queens, fought back. Three nights of rioting ensued which, to many, mark the birth of the gay rights movement in this country.

For the twentieth anniversary of the Stonewall Riots, in June 1989, I produced an oral history documentary, "Remembering Stonewall," which aired on Pacifica Radio and NPR's Weekend All Things Considered. The piece reconstructed the riots through the voices of the participants and presented the stories of others whose lives were changed by Stonewall. Two of the most memorable voices from the documentary were those of Sylvia (Ray) Rivera, a drag queen who was seventeen on the night of the riots and has since become something of a Rosa Parks figure for the gay rights movement, and Deputy Inspector Seymour Pine, the public morals squad officer who led the raid on the Stonewall that night.

In July 1994, five years after the documentary first aired, and a week after the celebrations surrounding the twenty-fifth anniversary of Stonewall, Harvey and I brought together Sylvia Rivera and Seymour Pine for a photograph at the site of the riots. It was the first time that the two had come face to face in twenty-five years. "I just want you to know that I respect you," Sylvia told Inspector Pine, shaking his hand. "I know you were just doing what you had to do." "Yeah," said Pine, shaking back firmly. "And I want you to know that it was never anything personal. We were never out to hurt you guys. Just doing our job."

SYLVIA RIVERA

Are we ready? Ooohhh, hello there! This is Sylvia Rivera—that's my drag name, and my real name is Ray Rivera Mendoza, and I've been a street person and a queen since the age of ten.

I was born in the Bronx at the old Lincoln Hospital, in the parking lot, in 1951. My moms wanted a Fourth of July baby, but the queen wanted to be born on July 2nd, so I was born feet first in a taxicab in the parking lot. Grandma raised me, because my mom committed suicide when I was three. Her second husband was a drug dealer, and she didn't want drugs in the house. He threatened to kill her and me, so the only way that she knew to cop out was she poisoned herself and she also tried to poison me at that time. When I got older my grandmother told me that one of her last wishes was that she wanted to kill me, because she knew somehow that I was gonna have a hard life. I gotta give the woman credit— she did know, because it's sure been hard.

My grandmother lived on the Lower East Side in a fifth-floor walk-up. She tried to give me a lot, but being who I was, I just

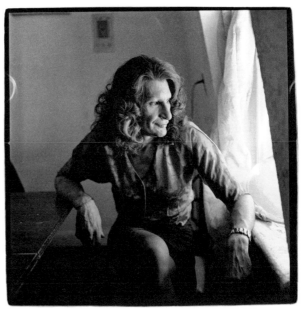

was not fitting in with the program. In fits of anger she would say, "I never wanted you, but I ended up with you and now I gotta deal with it." I was too effeminate, you know, I was too wild.

When we used to go on the subway, the adults would always start laughing when we got to Forty-second Street. The queens would get on and they'd say, "Oh, look at the patos"—which means "faggot"—and "This is where they all hang out." This is how I discovered Forty-second Street. One day I was curious, so I went. I was just hanging around and this man came up to me and offered me money, and I was like, "Okay, let's go." And I saw that you can make money by having sex with men. I was ten years old, and being that I was a young thing, there was actually very good-looking men picking me up, and I thought, "I can have sex and I can enjoy myself and I can make money, and get things that I want that my grandmother couldn't afford."

Things started getting out of hand when people from the neighborhood saw me on Forty-second Street hustling, and I was still living at home. They started making fun of my grandmother, calling her names and what-not. I remember that she came home crying one time saying, "Oh, they're calling me a pimp, and you're out there on Forty-second Street." That was the first time I tried to off myself. I took an o.d. of pills, and ended up in Bellevue Hospital. I was still ten. From there they put me in the state nut house, and tried to talk my grandmother into signing for me to have shock treatment. The only thing that saved me is that one of the woman attendants, that happened to be a gay woman, explained to her in Spanish that—"Look, it's not gonna do any good for him. He is who he is. Don't let these doctors talk you into doing this to him." And actually that's the only thing that saved me from becoming a vegetable today, because I saw too many people go through shock treatment when I was at the state hospital, and they might as well have been dead.

I ran away from the nut house, and I ended up on Forty-second Street and hustled and became part of the streets. But I still wasn't amongst the queens. The first queen that I met in my whole life was Marsha P. Johnson—the P stands for "pay it no mind". She was hustling on Sixth Ave and Forty-second Street, and I was coming across the way. She says, "Hey, girlie, come over here. I don't know you." And I said, "My name is Ray"—'cause I still hadn't gone under my drag name. "Well, Miss Ray, how old are you?" And I said, "I'm ten." And she says, "Well, you should be home with your mother, child." And I looked at her and I said, "Well, how old are you?" And she was sixteen, seventeen—I don't remember—so I said, "Well, *you* need to be home." And she said, "Miss Thing, are you hungry? I got some money—let's go eat." So we ended up going to eat at Romeo's Restaurant on Forty-second Street, and Marsha started introducing me to the other queens. And just to find a realm where there were some others like me, I felt more comfortable.

I actually got the name Sylvia just before I turned eleven. That was given to me by an old, old lesbian and an old, old drag queen. They went through the scenario of having me christened—they had a big party, and there was a Pentecostal minister that did the ceremony. The original name that they wanted to give me was Carmen, but I didn't want that name because that was my mother's name, and I didn't want to carry my mother's name. Sylvia just popped up because there was no Sylvias at that time, and they were trying to find a name that wasn't being too used. It's actually Sylvia Lee, because I always liked Lee. So when I was christened, it was as Sylvia Lee Rivera.

The community on Forty-second Street—we all basically stuck together. At that time I was the youngest of a group of forty or fifty drag queens. You know, we all slept in the movie houses—I mean in those days you could see two movies for forty-five cents and sleep all day and then go out and hustle. It was fun, but it was constant harassment. The police were always beating you up. I got beat up a couple of times by the cops on Forty-second Street for no reason at all. Straight bands of boys would also come to the Square and start beating up drag queens. Even your straight gay brothers—I mean main-stream gay people who copped out to wearing the suits and ties so they could be accepted—would come up and beat the living daylights out of a queen. But being that I was a queen, I learned to live with a lot of this.

We queens were all very tight, because we only had each other (and actually we still only have each other). The years passed, and we moved into what they called back then the "hot springs" hotels, that had "trick" rooms that the queens and the whores would rent for a half hour. We lived at the Aristo Hotel on Forty-third Street and Sixth Avenue, and we used to all sit around and say, "Someday we'll be free." We used to just dream—waiting for the revolution to come, hoping and wishing to be free. I guess as they say, or as Shakespeare says, we were "ladies in waiting," just waiting for the thing to happen. And when it did happen we were there.

I never thought I would be there when it happened. I actually never thought it would happen so quick. Normally the Stonewall was a hustlers' bar. A few drag queens went there, but the main drag queen bar was called the Washington Square Bar, and that was a few blocks away on Broadway. We went to the Stonewall that night, and we were havin' a good time. But the next thing you know the lights flash on, and the whole number. You know—"We're bein' raided again. Great!"

They started separating people, and let us leave the bar. Usually what we did was walk around the corner and have some coffee. The cops would padlock the door, take the liquor, and leave. The Mafia—the gay bars were all run by the Mafia—they would come around the corner five minutes later with the fucking watered-down liquor and a box of money, crack the door open, and they were back in business again a half hour later. But that night we didn't disperse from in front of that bar like we always did. We just stood outside. It was hot, and we were fed up. I know I was fed up. No one left the front of that bar. No one was going anywhere.

It started with people throwing pennies. Then the bricks and bottles started. Now, everybody says that it was me that threw the first bottle. No. It was somebody that was behind me that threw the first bottle. But when the first bottle went by me, I said, "Oh Lord Jesus, the revolution is finally here! Hallelujah—it's time to go do your thing!" Then all kinds of things started flying! I broke out of the crowd trying to find something to throw, and someone handed me a Molotov cocktail. I don't know where it came from, I had never handled one in my life, but it was lit and they said, "Hurry up and throw it." So I did, and boom! And then the cars started being turned over and glass started breaking.

From the two hundred or three hundred people that were standing out in front of the bar, it went through the neighborhood, and the Village lit up like a Christmas tree. Before you know it, it was thousands of fags and dykes! The brothers and sisters came out of the woodwork like fucking roaches, so help me God. I mean the street was covered! Where they came from, I don't know, but it seemed like everybody was waiting. I guess we were all tired. It was our time to join the revolution. The moment was there, and we seized it .

To be with all these people, all these brothers and sisters, to see everybody united on one front, was beautiful, it was really beautiful. I was no saint. I wanted to do every destructive thing that I could think of at that time to hurt anyone who had hurt us over the years. A lot of blood was shed, but people stood. They decided that they were gonna fight back, that nothing was going to stop them. I got knocked a coupla times. I got it across my back, across my legs, but I kept coming back for more and more. Everybody kept coming back for more. Even people that were covered in blood kept coming back for more. They said, "No. We're not giving up." And that's what made the night beautiful: nobody was afraid. Nobody was afraid that night to die.

The movement was born that night, and we knew we had done something that everybody in the whole world would know about when the news came out. They would know that gay people stood up and fought, and that would make everybody else stand up and fight. And even the next day there was an immediate change amongst the community—letting themselves be visible to the world. You saw lovers walking down the street holding hands and kissing in public. I mean, these were things that before you had to do late at night, when no one could see you. But in broad daylight! It was beautiful to see this. It was beautiful to see people not hiding. And that's when we knew that nothing was going to ever be the same again—at that time or at any time in the future.

I'm very proud that I was there, but I know that we have a long ways more to go, and the main thing is to keep fighting the fight.

Since Stonewall, Sylvia has worked a variety of jobs in food service, and has struggled with drug and alcohol addiction. She now lives in Yonkers, New York.

SEYMOUR PINE

Ah, I'm Seymour Pine, and I was born on July 21, 1919, and I was a member of the New York City Police Department for thirty-five years. When I was a young man, I wanted very much to get into the FBI. But at the time that was very diffi-cult for someone who is Jewish, so my father suggested that I go into the New York City Police Department. I went into the police department, and I was there for about five months before I went into the army—World War II.

I served in the army for four years—in Africa and Sicily, and in England, where I joined up with General Patton. During this time I authored a manual called *Hand to Hand Combat for the Infantry Soldier* which I believe is still in use in the army. I was severely wounded before the Battle of the Bulge. I was blown up in a mine, and for all intents and purposes that was the end of the war for me.

I came back and went back to the police department, and had what was known as a "light duty" job for two years, because I still had to get hospital treatment. I studied for sergeant and I passed that, and I passed the lieutenant's exam and the captain's exam. And I was captain in various precincts throughout the city, before I was promoted to deputy inspector in charge of public morals in 1964 or '65 at the Sixty-first Precinct right in the Mafia area in Bensonhurst. In the army I had done work in Sicily, and had a pretty good knowledge of the way the Mafia oper-ated. I also spoke Italian, so that was beneficial. I worked there for a couple of years, and then they decided that I would do better in Manhattan with the First Division, because that was the home of the Mafia. It included Greenwich Village, Little Italy, Chinatown—those areas that essentially housed all of the families.

Public Morals was a unit in each police division in the city that enforced the laws concerning vice and gambling, including prostitution, narcotics, and laws and regulations concerning homosexuality. We never, or almost never, made arrests of homosexuals, with the possible exception of the transvestites. They vio-lated a section of the penal code which dealt with masquerading—Section 240.35, paragraph 4: "Being masked or in any manner disguised by unusual or unnatural attire or facial alteration, loiters, remains or congregates in a public place with other people so masked or disguised, or knowingly permits or aids per-sons so masked or disguised to congregate in a public place; except that such con-duct is not unlawful when it occurs in connection with a masquerade party or like entertainment. . . ."

Now at that time, the Mafia ran all the gay clubs. The legitimate bars refused to admit homosexuals. If you went into a bar and sat down in a booth with a man and held hands, you were thrown out. You certainly couldn't get up and dance, and God forbid if you kissed—because their liquor licenses were in jeopardy!

This was under the Alcohol and Beverage Control Act, and the way the laws were written, they were really stacked against gay people. The Mafia saw the opportunity, you see, of exploiting the homosexuals. First of all, they were a good money source. Second of all, once they knew you were a homosexual, you were sort of at their mercy because of the bonding laws that were in existence at that time—that meant you couldn't work in an insurance company, banks, or any number of places if you were gay—and because of the attitude of many of the commercial institutions towards homosexuals. No one was protected by the law as far as that was concerned, and once you told the Mafia where you worked they had you in their clutches.

So raiding these clubs was another facet of my work. Typically, we'd send in two undercovers—usually females—and then just wait outside. They'd go in, and at the point that they had enough evidence, they would give us a signal—if there was a window they would just wave to us, or whatever. Then they'd walk up to the manager and say, "Okay, this is a raid. Turn the lights on." Which they did do, and "Everybody out! Have your IDs with you on the way out." It would've been an additional charge, you see, if they had been serving a minor, so we wanted to see their ID cards. And you felt two guys could handle two hundred people. You tell them to leave and they leave. You say, "Show me your identification," and they all take out their identification and file out—and that's it. And this was a kind of power that you had, and you never gave it a second thought.

We originally had word that the Stonewall was exploiting homosexuals who were working in the Wall Street area, and that they were being forced to give information to the Mafia. Negotiable bonds from some of the depositories were missing and had surfaced on the street. Whether it was Interpol or our own Stocks and Bonds Squad that came up with the information, I don't know—but they believed that it came from the homosexual-Mafia connection, and the only thing we could do was to try to break the connection between the two.

So that night we had decided that we would take the Stonewall. We sent in two police women—one was a big husky, and one was a very dainty looking female—and they looked like a perfect team. They got in, and they were supposed to spot all the people who were working there, and they were supposed to give us a signal when to come in. When we thought they were in there long enough and maybe they were in trouble, we went in. (It turned out nothing was wrong—maybe they were doing a little partying too.) We had no trouble getting in, and we immediately said, "Everybody get your identity cards out . . . " and that kind of thing, and we began moving people out. In the meantime, the people who were actually working in the club were put in the back room, and we began taking information from them—names and so forth. We also kept a couple of the transvestites who gave us flak. Everybody else—out! At this point it was a perfectly normal operation, no different from what we had been doing at the Stonewall or any other place. We gathered all the liquor together, and we started to go out. There was never any reason to feel that anything of an unusual situation would occur that night.

There was a patrol wagon outside, and we loaded that up with the people who worked in the place—not the transvestites, they were held back for the next wagon—and we told the driver to get back as soon as he could. We were just sorta waiting around on the street for the patrol wagon to come back when everything started. The crowd hadn't dispersed. They usually scooted away—they didn't scoot away. It was at that time, while we were waiting, that they started throwing pennies. That was the first thing. They were throwing coins, and calling names—none of which bothered us. There was no fear on our part, no apprehension that anything was going to happen. The only thing was that the crowd hadn't dispersed. As a matter of fact, it was growing.

Then a police officer was hit in the eye by a coin. I went into the crowd and grabbed the guy who threw it, and made the arrest. It was at that point the bottles and the stones and everything began to fly. And still no patrol wagon. We called over the radio, and we didn't get any response. I said to the officers, "Okay, everybody inside." And that's what we did—we went inside the Stonewall. We withdrew. We shut the doors and tried to barricade them with tables.

At that point all hell broke loose. They crashed all the windows, and started throwing in bricks and paving blocks. Then the Molotov cocktails started coming in—bottles with gasoline that were exploding. It was at that point that I realized that my men were very nervous, and I was very apprehensive. There was no way out—the windows in the back had been barred. We didn't know how many hundreds or thousands or whatever was outside, but we knew that if they got in, the only way we could contain them with the small number of men that we had was by shooting. We all had our guns drawn, and I kept saying, "Nobody shoot! Nobody shoot! Don't fire your gun—I'll be the first to shoot!" Remember, these were pros, but everybody was frightened, there's no question about that. I know I was frightened. I mean, I'd been in combat situations, but there was never any time I felt more scared than I felt that night.

We noticed a group of persons attempting to uproot one of the parking meters, which they did succeed. They then used that parking meter as a battering ram to break down the door, and they did in fact crash in the door. Then I was sure we were gonna have to fire, but I was very reluctant to give the order. I still kept saying: "Nobody fire! Let's back up if we have to. Help's gonna be coming." And, as luck would have it, just as they crashed through the door, we heard the sirens. For us, all the tension was gone: we knew we were safe because the Tactical Patrol Force, the riot squad, was coming in very large numbers.

To this very day, in trying to analyze why the hostility, there is no way else to explain it other than: "We've had enough!" We did nothing differently. We did the same obnoxious things to them that we did every time: we went in, and chased them out. But this time they didn't go. And after that, things were completely changed. From then on they were not submissive anymore. They now suddenly had gained a new type of courage, and it seemed as if they didn't care anymore whether their identities were made known. We were now dealing with human beings.

Seymour Pine retired from the New York City Police Department in 1976. Today he lives in Israel, where he volunteers as a police officer in Jerusalem. ■

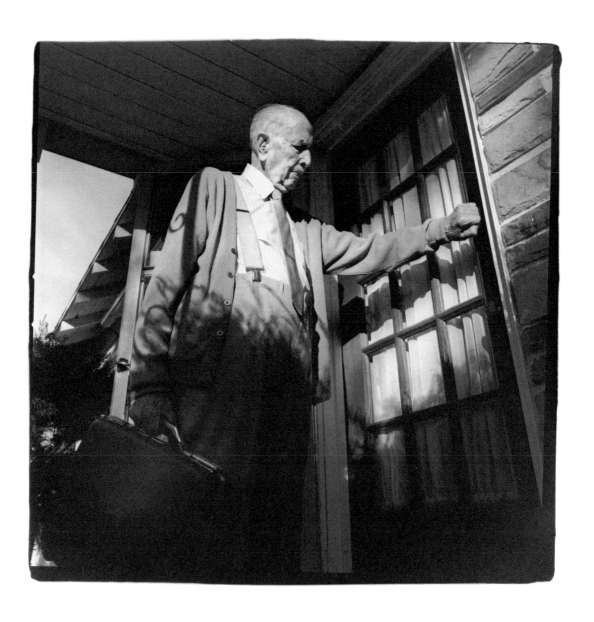

Mackey E. Brown
DOOR-TO-DOOR SALESMAN
SPOKANE, WASHINGTON

"If you give me a good product, inexpensive, I could work my way around the world with it, no money in my pocket," Mackey Brown told us in his room at the Good Samaritan Rest Home in Spokane. "I've canvassed over a million doors. Sold two million dollars in products: pianos, refrigerators, radios, TVs, washing machines, blankets, shoes, cookware—you name it, I sold it. Worked seventy-five years—that's the longest anyone has sold door-to-door in *history*. And I never saw a person I didn't like. Never."

When we met Mr. Brown in October 1993, he was eighty-five years old, and recovering from a debilitating stroke which had left his speech all but incomprehensible. Nonetheless, Mr. Brown was still hard at work—selling fire extinguishers door-to-door at the houses near his rest home. "I make the best of it," he told us. "I like people, and I like to talk. If you have a good product, you don't need to worry." ■

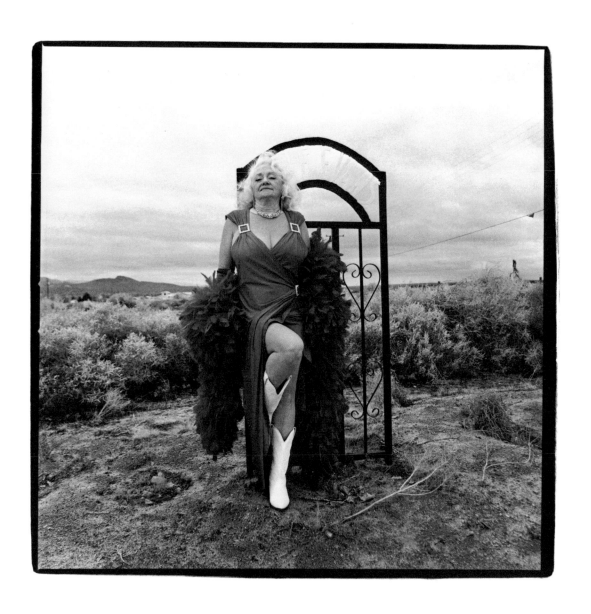

Dixie Evans
CURATOR, EXOTIC WORLD MUSEUM AND STRIPPER (RETIRED)
HELENDALE, CALIFORNIA

"The only burlesque historical society in the world" is housed in a converted goat-shed in California's high desert. "We're exactly halfway between Las Vegas and L.A., just a half mile off old Route 66," giggles Dixie Evans. "It's kind of hard to find, but you'd be surprised how they do get here."

Walk through a sliding glass door, and you've entered the first of five rooms that make up the museum: the "Hubba-Hubba Hall of Fame." The walls are covered with framed photographs of burlesque greats. Christmas lights blink. Mannequins in slinky dresses stand beside glass display cases filled with old pasties, G-strings, and handbills from the golden era of burlesque.

Dixie Evans, once known as "The Marilyn Monroe of Burlesque," watches over Exotic World—guiding visitors (about two a day), dusting the artifacts, and answering correspondence. She's run the museum since its founder, her friend Jenny Lee, "The Bazoom Girl," died of cancer in 1990.

I'm Dixie Evans, and I was born August the 28th, 1926, which makes me 66 years old—I'm the exact same age as Marilyn Monroe, just a few months difference. I've had a hankering to be in show business all my life—ever since I was little. My daddy—he was an oilman—used to have these big poker games when all the oilmen would get together. On break, I'd have already rigged up my costumes and I'd do my little dance and pass the hat around. They'd already had a couple of drinks by then, and boy, I'd make my little money and I'd run in the bedroom and hide it. And I could hardly wait for the next poker game, you know, 'cause I was in *show business!*

My father was killed when I was about eleven years old. My mother went into a terrible depression after he died and cried and cried, and I had to take care of her. We moved from having big expensive things to absolutely nothing—to a little room on Temple Street in Los Angeles with a hot plate and my mother still crying. My mother was really sweet, she was lovely. The only thing is she sat there with this blue chenille bathrobe, with cold cream crusted around her neck, and just cried all the time. I just knew something had to give sooner or later. So finally one day I just said "Mom, when that clock ticks, I'll be eighteen years old, and I'm leaving." She said, "Oh honey, don't leave me! Don't leave me!" Well, I left.

I got a job as a page in the theater—you walk out, open the curtain, then the big act comes through. A couple of times I worked in a burlesque theater as a page—and I said, "Wow! She's getting two hundred and fifty dollars a week, and she's about forty-five"—you know how you think when you're real young— "and here I am getting sixty five dollars. There's something wrong here!" So I'd kind of cozy up and get friendly with these stars—and they were stars—and couple of them helped me a lot.

I started in Oakland at a theater called the El Rey—that's where Tempest Storm broke in. Oh, the El Rey was great. The shows we put on were really good. People think a burlesque show was full of strippers. Oh no! There were twenty, thirty chorus girls coming out (or maybe six or ten depending on the size of the city) and they didn't do just one little number—they'd come out with costumes, then they'd fade in the wings and come back with hats—I mean, big production numbers! A lot of costumes, wardrobe, scenery. We had good light men, we had good sound technicians—everyone was working to make the show good, because if we were a success we were going to get paid and we were going to go another week. So that will give you an idea how professional the burlesque theaters were.

Burlesque comes from an Italian word *burlare* which means to laugh and have fun. And burlesque started over in England in the sixteenth century. Louie the . . . oh gosh, I don't know exactly which one, but they'd have the show and there were songs and funny skits and dances about wealthy people—and it was very chic for people to go and laugh and look at these skits. Then it came to America. "Lydia Thompson and her British Blondes." That was 1861, I think. It was just music hall—crazy little songs and British blondes in tights—but America had never seen girls run out in tights. One time, a girl by the name of Hinda Wassau was doing an act where she had an outer garment and an undergarment. Between acts she had to run offstage to take her outer dress off and do a dance in the beaded dress underneath. Well, her beads got all tangled and she couldn't get the darn dress off backstage. Her other music was coming on, so the stagehands just shoved her out onstage. So she had to wiggle out of the outer dress onstage to the music. The audience was goin' crazy—they actually got to see somebody undress in front of them—nobody'd ever thought of it before! So the producers said, "Uh-huh. This is where it's at." So striptease is an American original.

Every city in the United States had at least two or three burlesque theaters— even on the West Coast, we had 'em here. The Old Howard in Boston was "the first and the oldest," they used to say. The fellows at Harvard couldn't get their diploma unless they'd gone to the Old Howard. [Laughs] And Lily St. Cyr had played there and Tempest Storm and myself—and on Friday nights you'd get the college kids, oh gosh, they'd hoot and holler. They'd try to be very sophisticated at first, but then when the comedian comes on or something funny happens, well then they couldn't hold it any longer and they'd say, "What the hell—this is kinda good!" [Laughs]

We all looked up to Lily St. Cyr as the greatest. Even Tempest Storm looked up to Lily St. Cyr. Sensational! In one number she did, she'd stroll onstage loaded with big hat boxes and boxes of clothes—everything she bought that day. She'd begin to disrobe, and the phone would ring and she'd just hang up on him. Then she'd continue to disrobe to music and lights and bubbles, and then the phone would ring again, and she'd hang up on that one. Then all of a sudden you could tell by the music when the phone rang that this was the one she wanted to talk to. She'd be on the telephone and swirl on the couch—and I mean, the moves! So it told a story—this was the man that she was in love with. Then she'd be totally nude, but hiding behind the couch. Then she'd go up these gorgeous glass stairs, way up to the top, and into this beautiful glass bathtub, and bubbles would come out and her washrag was ostrich plumes and stones and everything. Then she'd step out, and then there'd be a red overhead spotlight, and she'd do quite a little shimmy dance drying off with a beautiful towel. Then she'd come down these stairs—real, real elegant. A maid would come on and give her a dress. She'd put on a gorgeous chiffon gown, do a real great dance, and then she'd whip it off—she didn't want to wear that dress! Then the maid would bring out another one, and then she'd do a fantastic act in that gown—and she didn't like that gown! Then all of a sudden the maid would bring out a gold lame, and you knew that was the one. Then the maid would bring a big mink coat (oh, a *gorgeous* mink coat), and put it on her. You'd see a man's white gloves and flowers peeking out, and that would be the end—she'd go stroll offstage.

My numbers were all production numbers too. They called me "the Marilyn Monroe of Burlesque." And Marilyn was very upset with me for doing that—she tried to sue me. I had an agent out of New York who booked all the shows, and I liked seeing my name up on the marquee. Then one day I went to the Carmen Theater in Philadelphia—they had a great big theater with a fourteen-piece band—and I look up there and there's "air conditioning" in real big letters on the marquee. That was then end of our names on the marquee. We had to settle for "air conditioning."

When Marilyn died, I went into the most horrible depression. I couldn't believe it. I had just done a show in Connecticut. I was married to a professional prizefighter at the time, and he came into my bedroom and said "Dixie, Marilyn's dead." I jumped out of bed like a wild animal, and I pounded my fist in his chest and said, "Don't you do that to me! I hate you! I hate you!" And he grabbed my wrist and said, "Dixie, Marilyn's dead." Then he led me to the living room, and the TV was rolling about Marilyn and I couldn't believe it.

I went into *the* worst depression. I was booked two years in advance. All of a sudden, I was totally canceled. You feel like you're dead—you just *die*. It was horrible! The only other person in the world who would realize what I went through was Vaughn Meader. Now Vaughn Meader did Kennedy, President Kennedy. And Kennedy had him to the White House, and Kennedy would just roll on the floor laughing and hollering. Vaughn Meader was on the Ed Sullivan show, pulling down *big* money. Then all of a sudden that happened to him. I was at the B&G coffee shop (it used to be Hanson's Drugstore), and I remember seeing Vaughn after Kennedy died, these big soulful eyes in this black cashmere coat and his black hat, and the rain was pouring down, and he was just staring. He was lost. He was finished. Last thing I heard he was wandering the hills of Tennessee—he didn't care about anything, anybody—nothing! Marilyn hadn't died yet when I saw Vaughn Meader out in front of the B&G on Broadway. Then, when it happened to me, all of a sudden I could just see Vaughn Meader with the rain pouring down.

Burlesque was the only thing that was ever good to me. After my father died, my mother didn't laugh and my sister and I weren't permitted to laugh—it was "disrespectful." But when I got to burlesque I found a bunch of crazy wonderful girls who liked to laugh and laugh. See, these pictures on the walls are not just photographs. To me they're real-life girls who went through struggles. We'd get paid on Wednesday—our draw—you'd always draw half your salary on Wednesday in case the show folds. A girl would say, "Come on, I got to wire fifty dollars to my mom"—her mom would be a drunk or something. And I knew so many girls that struggled and struggled, and every penny they made they'd send home. This is my family, see. These girl's names will *not* be forgotten! They will not! ■

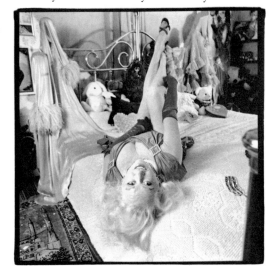

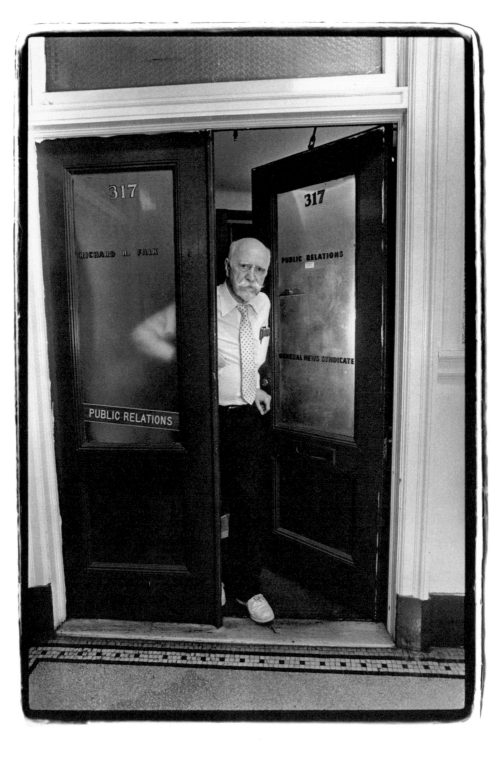

Dick Falk
Press Agent
New York City

It was the winter of 1991. I was having a tough time coming up with story ideas. I was feeling bleak. I thought I might do something about death. On a lark, I looked up "Funeral Directors" in the yellow pages. Near the top of the A's a listing caught my eye: "Airplane Ashes." I called the number, and Dick Falk answered. "They call me the Pilot of Death," he told me, sounding like he might fall out of his chair with excitement. "I'm listed in the phone books as an undertaker, but actually I'm an

'overtaker'—I don't take people down, I take them up."

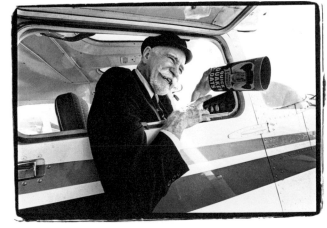

Dick Falk, as it turned out, had been sprinkling people's ashes out of airplanes for two decades. He had the routine down pat. First the crematorium would send the ashes to his Forty-second Street office. Then Falk transfered the ashes from the cremator's plain brown packaging into what he considered a more suitable receptacle. ("Actually I put them in what's known as an oatmeal box. Why? Because it fits!") He'd scrawl the client's vital statistics on top of that box, rent a plane and scatter the ashes over the spot the deceased had specified.

Several weeks after our initial phone call, Harvey and I flew with Dick Falk as he sprinkled the ashes of a woman named Mabel over the Statue of Liberty. According to her oatmeal lid, she was a secretary from St. Louis who died at the age of eighty-two. "It's fascinating, these people who send me their ashes," he told us. "What they were! Their stories, their lives! They worked, they loved, they had children! And now they're simply reduced to two and a half pounds of bone in an oatmeal box!" At one point, caught up in the excitement of the moment, Dick acci-

dentally spilled Mabel onto my notebook. He brushed her back into the oatmeal box with a dramatic sweep of the hand. Good radio story.

It turned out, though, that there was much more to Dick Falk than Airplane Ashes, which was really just a sideline business for him, a chance to use his amateur pilot's license to make a little extra money and generate some publicity. For more than half a century, Falk has staked a claim as one of Broadway's great press agents, pulling every preposterous stunt imaginable to land his clients in the papers. Falk insists he was the model for the evil flack Sidney Falco from the classic film The Sweet Smell of Success *(although he comes across as more of a* Broadway Danny Rose*).*

In September 1991, Harvey and I showed up at Falk's office to interview him about his career. At the time, Falk's handful of clients included a poet who was about to run for the presidency on the Mental Liberation ticket, and Angie Dickinson's astrologer.

Falk was also the only tenant remaining in a building slated to be torn down as part of a Times Square redevelopment project. He refused to move. "I'm suing for four hundred and fifty-five thousand," he told us, amid the press-release-strewn wreckage of his second-floor office. "It'll take that much to replace this place. What are they offering me—ten thousand? I mean come on, come close!" We spoke with Dick for about two hours, and then told him it was time to take a photograph. Falk pulled a tie out of an envelope on the floor, and Harvey made the picture.

Hello. My name's Dick Falk and my office is on Times Square in Manhattan. I get mail that just says "Dick Falk, New York City"— all the carriers know me. I've been eight-tenths of my life what they call a "flack"—a press agent. Everybody asks me sometimes, "What's the difference between a press agent, a publicity bureau and a public relations man?" Well, a press agent normally handles one client at a time—he gets his whole salary from that star or that show. A publicity bureau is a mimeograph house that turns out press releases, and a public relations man is sort of a "super" person that is over everything—he doesn't sit down and write releases or pull stunts like jumping off a building with a parachute—he's actually *over* the advertising people. So that's the division of the three. And I'm the last living press agent. It's a strange world, really. Colorful. Very colorful.

I started in the business when I was young. I was nineteen, and I actually got pretty good accounts because I was eager. When I first came here I did all my business from a telephone booth on Broadway. I put a telephone booth on my letterhead, and I put the hours when I would be standing by my booth, and I would just hang around waiting for calls, and if somebody else got in it, I'd just wait till they got out. It was so cheap! Later I got a little office on Forty-third and Eighth Avenue and I moved into this office about twenty years ago.

My clients? I've dealt with every celebrity of the age, practically. I can run through 'em: Barbra Streisand, Salvador Dalí, Shubert Brothers, Pat Suzuki, Dana Andrews, Sonja Henie, Milton Berle, Rudy Vallee, Dave Brubeck, Sally Rand, the Gabors, Charlotte Von Vote (no one actually knows who she is—I'm just throwing her in to get a free plug) Tallulah Bankhead, Jacqueline Susann. These are all personalities I handled—I handled every one of them! They all came to me. I said, "What do you want?" They said, "Make me famous!" Take Streisand for instance—she can't read a note (she can sing, of course) she can't act, and yet the world accepts her as the greatest. I uncovered her, I started her, I pushed her and I promoted her. Then, when all the maniacs trying to make money out of her came in, I dropped her like a hot potato. I didn't want to run around guiding these people to become superstars—they kill you! They demand your energy, your soul. I know one guy got killed—good friend, big press agent.

He was in a car with a couple of top superstars and they were forcing the driver to go so fast that they drove right into the river—they all died. If you had a dollar for every press agent that was killed because they catered to these crazy stars . . .

I've handled some very unusual accounts.

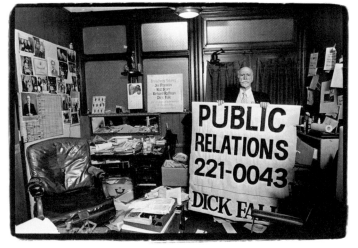

One time when it was slow I made a little airplane out of a release that said, "I'm a Publicist Ready for Clients" and I threw it out my window. A woman picked it up and came up to talk to me. She had this comb and it had a bulb at the end of it. There was holes in the teeth, and when you squeezed it flea powder would come out of the hole. It was for combing a dog: squeeze it and the flea powder goes on his head. I did a big story on it, and got the account. People buy it! I had this cemetery in New Jersey. They had an office in New York where they had this little grave with a tombstone on it and all kinds of flowers to show what they're selling. To get publicity, I'd have a press conference and give away a free gravesite to some famous person. They were glad to get it—I mean, if you're going to go, why not get a free grave?

There was a show, a comedy, that I was a press agent for, about a boy that lost his eyes, his ears, his nose, his arms and his legs—and he's in this little glass jar. He only could communicate by vibrating—he used to vibrate, and they find out that his little vibrations would spell out words like "hungry." That was a *comedy* that I was the press agent for. What do you send out—a picture of the boy? I mean, no paper will use it! Oh Jesus, I mean I had some weird shows. I don't know. They'd just hire me for these unusual things.

You got to have sort of an elastic mind to be a press agent. First of all, you got to know what the public wants. They don't want to read that somebody got an 'A' in school—I mean, forget it! I represented the Peekskill Military Academy. I had a story that a Chinese boy that went to the academy got a hundred in one of his courses. I sent it out, and the editors called me back and said: "Please don't clutter our files with this nonsense." Then I sent out a story that the same little boy was a spy teaching them espionage—broke every paper in the country. And the Peekskill Military Academy fired me because the mothers come running up to take their children out. But then six months later, they couldn't take all the people—all the children wanted to be a spy. That was a tough case. ■

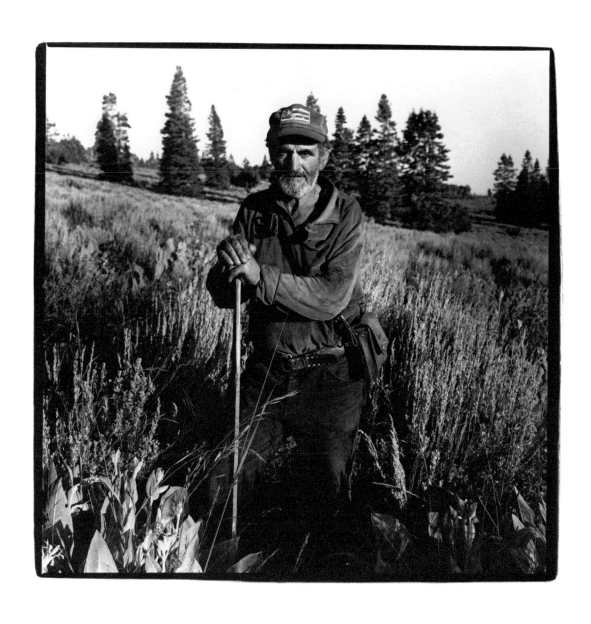

Segundo Mugarra
Basque Sheepherder
Warner Mountains near Madeline, California

Candido Olano and his partner, Segundo Mugarra, are two of the most difficult men in America to find. For both Harvey and me (we visited separately), tracking down these shepherds was a several-day ordeal involving remote dirt roads, destroyed transmissions, and deep feelings of hopelessness. We were finally able to locate them by pulling over to the side of the road and listening for the sound of sheep.

Candido and Segundo are the last remnants of a rich tradition of sheepherders which dates back to the 1850s. For more than a hundred years, almost all of the men plying the lonely trade in the American West were Basque immigrants from the mountainous region where France and Spain join, driven from their native land by poverty and war. Since the 1970s, however, the number of Basque shepherds in this country has been in rapid decline—largely because of changes in American labor regulations and improvements in the Basque economy. Today almost all of the Basque sheepherders have been replaced by immigrants from Mexico, Peru, and Chile.

For the past twenty-three years straight, Candido Olano has lived on the open range, grazing his flock along the same route each year: a 250-mile round-trip journey from California's Warner Mountains in the summer to Nevada's Lava Bed Mountains in the winter and back again. For the last fourteen years he's been accompanied by Segundo Mugarra. Mugarra speaks no English and preferred not to be interviewed. He was willing to be photographed, though, and Harvey took his picture in August 1993. I spent several hours with Candido Olano late one afternoon in June 1993, surrounded by four thousand bleating sheep. Dark-skinned and weathered-looking, a thick gray stubble on his face, Candido wore clothing caked with dirt, but his eyes sparkled. He spoke with a thick Basque accent.

CANDIDO OLANO

Jesus Christ! You come from the New York City? Oh boy! Jesus Christ! I be damned! Myself, I start here about 1958. Twenty-four of November. Young man. Myself is sixty-four now. Love the sheep. I think I born in a sheep barn in the old country. My mom never tell me where I born, so I think in a barn for I love sheep like that.

Pretty tough life here, really. Nobody likes much. Sleepin' in the brush, sleepin' on the ground. Climbin' the rocks, goin' down the rocks, sleepin' on the rocks. Sometimes you watchin' the rattlensakes round, round and round. One time I got in my neck one rattlesnake bite. Right there. Now it's a little different but first time coming to United States myself I got one donkey and no more. I sleep in a rocky place like nothin'—dropping my sleeping bag and sleep right there. Sometime pretty damn cold. Lot of times like that! Eat bread and drink a couple glasses wine and go to sleep. Sometime I put right here my teepee and go to bed. It start snowing—blowin' like hell with the snow! Come six or seven inches of snow on top my tepee. I stay in there nice, sleepin' like one baby. In the morning my teepee is fall down. I stick out my head and is coming one bunch of snow inside my bed! Oh boy! Colder than hell! Jesus Christ! I jump out of bed, put on the pants, and start making fire right there. . . . Tough, tough life. But Basco people I guess born pretty tough. Yeah, I think so.

I tell you, slow, slow, slow here. Years is going and years is coming and years is going. But I love sheep. It's my life like that. Young time, I tell you something, I love girls too. But now at my age, I think it's better love my sheep. . . . So I happy. Happy all the time. Most of the time singing some kind of songs. Like sometimes I go just singing like this:

> Mendian sortu nintzen
> Mendia det maite
> Ez naizela biziko
> Menditik aparte

I say like that in English:

> I born in the mountains.
> I love the mountains.
> I will never go
> out of the mountains.

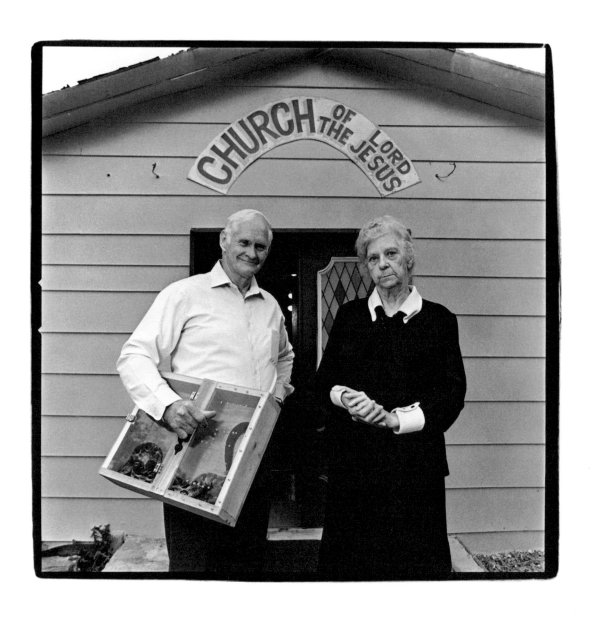

Dewey Chafin and his mother, Barbara Elkins
SERPENT HANDLERS
JOLO, WEST VIRGINIA

"Why I do it is because the Bible says to do it, and that's just the bottom line," Dewey Chafin explains as we trudge up a remote snake-infested hill in search of rattlesnakes and copperheads. "The Bible says, 'They shall take up serpents,' so I'm just doing what God told me to do."

Chafin is fifty-nine years old. He's a soft-spoken retired coal miner who's been handling serpents in church now for nearly thirty-five years. "Been bit one hundred and sixteen times—you'll keep count of that!" he tells me, holding up his hands for inspection. "See that finger? It came off with a copperhead bite. And when a rattlesnake bit me there, that thumb deteriorated—just rotted off! I got bit here with an Eastern diamondback sixty-two inches long—the finger swelled so big the skin just busted wide open. Both my hands are crippled. I can use them, but they're all bent out of shape."

Dewey leans forward on the old golf club he uses at a snake hook and points to a nearby rock "I found twenty-three copperheads under that one right there." I suggest we call it a day. Dewey keeps walking. A few minutes later, near the top of the mountain, he spots his prey—a black rattlesnake lying coiled and still on top of a rock. Dewey tries to pick it up with his golf club but the snake begins to glide away. Dewey grabs it with his hands. "I got him." Dewey says, dropping the snake into a burlap sack. "Not too big, but that'll kill you!"

> And these Signs shall follow them that believe;
> In my name shall they cast out devils; they shall speak
> with new tongues; they shall take up serpents; and if they
> drink any deadly thing it shall not hurt them;
> they shall lay hands on the sick and they shall recover.
> —Mark 16:17–18

Serpent handling dates back to 1909, when a Tennessee preacher named George Hensley had a revelation after reading this passage. He caught a rattlesnake, brought it into his church, and passed it around among his congregants. No one was injured, and serpent handling was born.

Hensley spent the next forty-five years preaching serpent handling throughout Appalachia. One of the believers whom Hensley converted was a young woman from Jolo, West Virginia, named Barbara Elkins—Dewey Chafin's mother. A few years later, she and her husband, Robert, along with Dewey, established the

Church of the Lord Jesus in their hometown. Barbara Elkins (who is now in her late seventies), Robert, and Dewey all continue to handle serpents in church. George Hensley died from a rattlesnake bite in 1955.

Jolo, West Virginia, is an unincorporated community of run-down houses and mobile homes nestled deep in the Appalachian Mountains. It was, at one time, a coal town, until all of its mines tapped out in the 1960s. Today Jolo is almost entirely populated by retired miners. There's not much to the place: one honky-tonk, a place to eat (the Hemlock Restaurant), and several places of worship, including the serpent-handling church.

The Church of the Lord Jesus, a simple yellow-painted wooden building, sits in the middle of a gravel parking lot at the edge of town. The inside is surpris-

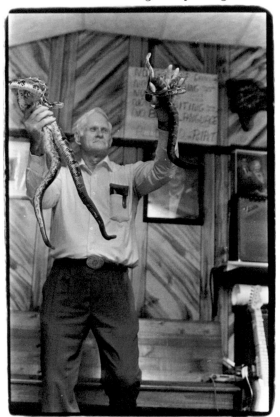

ingly modern. The hardwood floors are well polished, the plywood paneling on the walls looks new, clean white ceiling fans spin overhead.

Services are held three times a week: Friday and Saturday nights and Sunday morning. The dozen or so congregants are prompt. The women wear simple dresses, hair tied up in a bun. The men wear suits. Some arrive with musical instruments, others carry the simple wooden boxes that contain the serpents. The tops of these boxes are clear plastic, riddled with airholes. The sides are painted with the words LORD JESUS or PRAISE THE LORD. They're placed at the front of the church on the floor beside Pastor Bob Elkins, who runs the service. "I guess it's about time we got started," Elkins says to quiet the crowd. "These serpents are new serpents and we're not responsible for anybody that gets bit. If you handle them, you handle them on your own. If you get bit, you get bit on your own. Let's everybody pray."

With that, the members of the church drop to their knees, and begin praying aloud—a babble of voices, many speaking in tongues. Several minutes later, Pastor Elkins straps on a guitar and begins to sing. The congregants rise and join him. Before long, most make their way from the pews to the bare patch of floor at the front of the church and begin to dance.

The intensity of the service escalates. Before long the congregants are whirling around faster and faster, stomping across the wooden floor, scowling and sweating. Soon, a clean-cut young man wearing a Jesus beltbuckle moves toward a box of serpents. He bends down, opens the lid, and gently pulls out two rattlesnakes. He holds them up, stares at them, and begins to dance again. He lets them slither through his hands, and then passes one off to another congregant. The other boxes are opened, and soon a half-dozen snakes are being danced with and passed around. Barbara Elkins watches motionlessly from the front of the church, a deadly-serious expression frozen on her face. Soon, she too takes up a serpent and begins to dance. Women and men tremble and cry. Suddenly, the congregants return the serpents to their boxes and go back to their seats.

The service goes on like this for three hours. There's no order, no rules. Pastor Elkins alternately preaches to the congregation and leads them in song or prayer. When the service reaches a certain level of intensity the congregants pull out snakes or take a swig from a jelly jar that's filled with strychnine (congregants call it a "salvation cocktail").

In the five services I attended, no one was bitten or became sick from drinking the strychnine. Indeed, despite the fact that serpent handlers refuse medical treatment when bitten, in the eighty-year history of the practice there have been fewer than seventy confirmed deaths from poisoning.

Two of the deaths occurred in the Jolo church. One in 1991, when a believer named Ray Johnson was struck twice by a rattlesnake on the left wrist and died thirteen hours later. His widow and children continue to handle serpents each week. The other fatality occurred in 1962 to Barbara Elkins's daughter and Dewey Chafin's sister, Columbia Chafin. She was twenty-two years old. "It was on a Sunday about seven o'clock when she got bit," Dewey remembers. "The service started good. She just felt good, and she opened the box. It bit her while she was getting it out of the box and it hung onto her. She lived till Thursday. She died Thursday at five o'clock. We buried her Saturday. We went back to church the next weekend, handling serpents the same way. That's what she would have wanted."

There's been a fair amount of research into religious serpent handling. Those who've studied the services confirm that the snakes are neither defanged nor milked of their venom. There are any number of theories as to why the practice hasn't proved more deadly. Some researchers believe that the loud music played during the services subdues the snakes, or that the handlers enter a trance state which allows them to hold the animals without the sort of fear which normally induces the snakes to strike. Researchers agree that when believers are bitten, their bodies are somehow able to process the venom differently. No one is sure how or why—except the serpent handlers. "It's all up to God," explains Dewey Chafin. "If God wants me to live, I'll live."

Serpent handlers have faced a good deal of persecution over the last eighty years. Believers are ridiculed in their communities, or paraded around as freaks and cult members on afternoon talk shows. Their churches are regularly vandalized, their snakes stolen or killed as high school pranks. The practice has been outlawed in every Southern state except West Virginia and Georgia.

There have even been questions about the scripture upon which serpent handling is based. Most biblical scholars agree that the verse from Mark which tells believers to "take up serpents" was not originally part of the Bible, but was added much later by scribes attempting to give the book a more dramatic ending. The serpent handlers have heard this claim and aren't bothered by it a bit. "It can't be so," explains Dewey Chafin. "If that part was added, any part could have been added. I just don't believe it. Under no circumstances." Dewey pauses for a moment. "You know, when my time comes to die, that's the way I'd like to go— with a snake bite. That's just how I feel about it. I've felt that way for years." ■

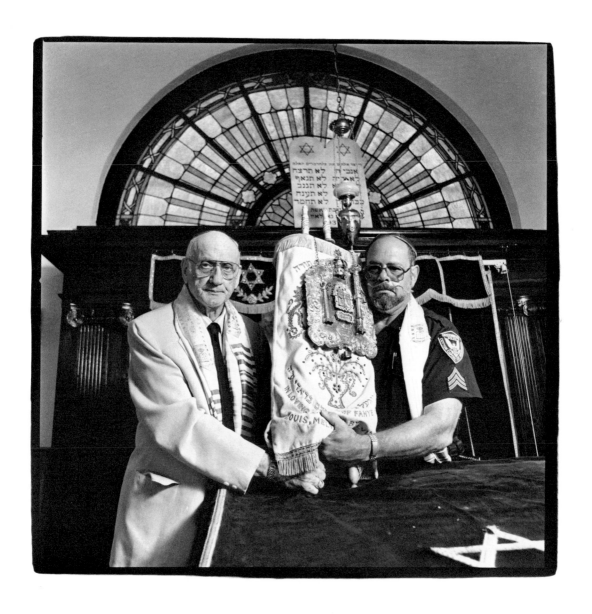

Leslie Kornfeld, President
and Joe Erber, Acting Rabbi
AHAVATH RAYIM SYNAGOGUE, GREENWOOD, MISSISSIPPI

Almost every Friday at about 7:45 P.M., auxiliary police officer Joe Erber calls in '10-6' (or 'busy') to his dispatcher. He cruises over to West Market Street on the outskirts of downtown Greenwood, Mississippi, and strides into Ahavath Rayim, the last Orthodox synagogue in the state. Erber grabs a prayer shawl off a rack, kisses it, and drapes it over his uniform. He makes his way to the pulpit and begins the services. Hebrew with a drawl.

For years now, Erber has served as the de facto rabbi of Ahavath Rayim, spiritual leader to a once-thriving congregation that has dwindled down to almost nothing. It's a story that can be found in small communities throughout the South. At the turn of the century, Jewish immigrants poured into towns like Greenwood seeking relief from the stifling tenement life up North. They arrived as peddlers, saved money, opened up stores. By the 1930s, Jews formed the backbone of the merchant class in hundreds of these towns. Soon after, though, young Jewish people began leaving, opting for the larger cities. By the early 1950s this small-town Jewish exodus was in full swing. Today, it's nearly complete.

In November 1991 I spent several days in the city of Greenwood with the remaining members of Ahavath Rayim. Leslie Kornfeld is the president of the synagogue and proprietor of Kornfeld's, one of only two Jewish-owned stores left in town. Joe Erber, auxiliary policeman and spiritual leader of Ahavath Rayim, is also a full-time postman in Greenwood. A six-foot-two, three-hundred-pound chain-smoker, he's not your typical yeshiva boy.

Watching Erber, a walkie talkie and billy club on one hip, a .357 magnum on the other, lead Friday-night services in Ahavath Rayim was a perfect moment. ("He keeps us all in line" Leslie Kornfeld whispered with a chuckle, elbowing his son, Bubba.) Before him were the dozen or so diehard congregants, most in their seventies or older. Erber's eyes were closed as he rocked back and forth in front of the simple mahogany ark that held the Torahs, the tassels of his prayer shawl lightly brushing the podium. I'd never felt prouder to be a Jew.

LESLIE KORNFELD

I'm Leslie Kornfeld, and I've just had my seventy-ninth birthday. I am a Jewish man. I was born here and lived here all my life. This is Kornfeld's Incorporated, what they call a "small business company." We sell children's, ladies', and men's clothes, but more or less we principally furnish the "big and tall" man. My father started this business years and years ago. It hasn't moved. We were here when the streets was mud and dirt. We've seen 'em come and we've seen 'em go.

I'd say at one time there must have been in this town alone fifteen or twenty or more businesses run by Jewish people. Today there's only two of us—Goldberg's and us are the only ones left. There used to be a lot of Jewish people that had little small stores. Used to be four or five across the street, and Diamond, my uncle, next door. And on the next corner was one, and further down was two more stores. And in the main part of town there was Aaronson's Shoe Store and Goodman's. And the Davidsons and the Watermans had stores here. Goldberg's, and Piltz, and Starr Tailors. And the Bennets had two stores here, and the Lanskys had two or three stores here. . . . Oh, just a bunch of them scattered around! And all the small towns was the same way: the dry goods store was mostly Jewish. They came here from up North, and got into a little town where it wasn't expensive, and they worked themselves up. I call them mom-and-pop stores, and they made a good living. But it's a forgotten world in that respect. Goldberg's and us are the last, and I doubt if my son will take it over—it's a lot of headache for one person.

I been president of the synagogue, I don't know how long. My cousin's father was president before me, and my father was president too—that's been a long time ago. I done lost track of the time. But in the olden days, we used to fill up the synagogue full! The shul used to be *packed* on the High Holidays, and we used to bring in chairs because we didn't have enough seats, it was so crowded. Folks used to come from within a radius of seventy-five or eighty miles away—Coffeeville, Grenada, Sunflower, Indianola, Belzona, Moorehead, Slaughter—all these little towns had two, three Jewish families. And on the High Holidays they came to *pray.* You might not but see 'em once a year, but they *came* on the High Holidays. They saw to it that they closed up shop and came to shul and begged God for forgiveness, and then we'd see them again maybe next year. [Laughs]

It wasn't too easy growing up here, because you had a mark on you. People in those days didn't understand—they look at you as a *Jew.* They look at you as if you wasn't a human being almost. I had fights. I was called "Christ killer." I told 'em, "What the hell did I have to do with killing Christ?" But afterwards, when I got to high school, I was center on the basketball team, I made the track team, and we got along fine. They looked at me and said, "Well, he's a human being after all, maybe!" [Laughs] You had a label on you in the old days, but that's been torn off.

We are supposed to be the only Orthodox shul in Mississippi, and I believe it is. What happened? Well, the older people died out. The young people went to college, got degrees—lawyers, doctors. They didn't want to go back to the little towns. You take a town with fifteen hundred people, a thousand or three thousand—these little communities around here. What have you got? A dry goods store and a grocery store and maybe a drugstore. No! There's nothing there for 'em. So they went either to Memphis or New Orleans or Birmingham—to the city—where they had a chance to do something. They had no chances here, no entertainment. Very few young Jewish boys, very few young Jewish girls. Who are they going to go with? They want to bring up their children in a Jewish way. You go to a little town like Moorehead or some place. Where you gonna find a good lox and bagel sandwich? No! A good kosher beef sandwich? No! You go where you have what you want. So they migrated. And they left us old folks here to ponder the future, and dream about the past.

It's really a pitiful situation, and it's not gonna get any better—it's just gonna get worse. I would never have thought that I'd live to see the day that we'd have eight or ten people on a Friday night. Men *and* women. I think of my daddy and my uncle and all those people who helped build the shul—they never would have thought this would happen. Never! But that's the way, as they say, the cookie crumbles. It's very disheartening to be honest with you. We just hope and pray God gives us a miracle. Maybe some families will move in here. I'd like to plead for a lot of Jewish families to move down here. If these good folks want to retire to a good place, tell 'em to come on down to Greenwood—we can use 'em! [Laughs] Give 'em free membership at the synagogue for a whole year! [Laughs] Because I'm seventy-nine, my wife is seventy. Sammy Kaplan is older than I am, and one of the Lansky boys is older than I am. If we lose any more, this'll go just like the Reform temple went. You know they had a Reform temple here too? They got to where there was three or four families left and they just sold the building. It's not even here anymore—it's a parking lot now. It's a tragic circumstance, when I think of it. . . . But we keep pluggin' along.

JOE ERBER
My name is Joe M. Erber. I'm fifty years old. I was born in Columbia, Tennessee, and I've lived in Greenwood since I was one year old. Most people call me Joe, but my mother, *olov hasholem* [rest in peace], called me Joe Martin, so the Yehudim all call me Joe Martin. I been part of the congregation now forty-nine years. I was taken to shul since the age of one year old, I'm sure. I don't remember, but I know my mother was there every time the door opened.

At one time there was an awful lot of Jewish folks in the city of Greenwood. I can remember the *shoykhet* coming to my grandmother's house and slaughtering the chickens in the backyard. All the women would come in, and they would prepare the meat with kosher salt, and take it home. I remember the . . . what do you call those beggars? The *meshulekhs*, the beggars. It's not a nice word, but they represent the yeshivas—very Orthodox Jewish people that traveled with the full *payus* and the beards. I remember one gentleman in particular. The only place he would eat was at my grandmother's house, and he wouldn't eat anything but a boiled egg and a banana because he was so Orthodox that nobody's food was kosher enough for him. He smoked Pall Malls, which were nonfiltered cigarettes, and he would let 'em burn up in that beard to a stub. I've never seen anybody smoke a cigarette down that short. And my brother and I used to just stand there and stare into his face to see when he was gonna catch that beard on fire. [Laughs] I remember those gentlemen and their begging—they'd come to Greenwood and approach all the Jewish people for donations, and then somebody from the congregation would have to put 'em on the bus so they could go on to the next town.

I can remember a time here in Greenwood when the rabbi would read something and the congregational response was almost deafening—like a roar. Now you hardly hear anything. At one time our Sunday School probably had two hundred, two hundred and fifty kids in it. Now we have two boys and two girls. If we can get ten men, a minyan, on Friday nights, we're well satisfied. We've had the service with five men or sometimes less present. When you don't have a minyan, you're not supposed to say certain parts of the service, but we're not gonna follow the rules that close. My late uncle and I used to call people and ask 'em to come to services, but we decided we'd quit—it just seemed like an imposition to ask someone when they know it's there for them. Still, if we have nine and somebody needs to say Kaddish, we'll get on the phone to try and find a tenth. . . . I've thought about how to say this for half a day now, going back and forth at work. . . . It's just that this *was* something. It was something to see, and something to be proud of. I'm not ashamed of it now, by any means, I don't mean that. But . . . It's just a ghost of what it was—it's a shadow.

Everybody has come to me at one time or another to say thank you for carrying on services. I say the Jewish religion is based on *mitzvahs*, and a *mitzvah* means doing a good thing. To me it's a *mitzvah* to do this. I fell into the job of trying to lead services when our president, Mr. Louis Brody, developed Alzheimer's disease. He led the services in Hebrew, and when he got to the point that he just didn't know where he was, somebody had to take over, and I ended up with it. Well, my dad had died just before that, so he never saw me lead services. But my mother did, and it brought a smile to her face to see her son up there doing what her father did, because my grandfather also helped to lead services. She was proud of me. And to me it was a tribute to her and the generations before to try to keep this going.

I don't lead a perfect Jewish life by any means, but the shul has always been *there*. It's just a part of my life. To lose it would be just like losing a member of my family—I can't put it any other way. It would be a sorrow. It's a part of my history. I can walk into shul and close my eyes and I can see my family sitting there. It's just so easy to do. My father had a hearing aid in both ears, and we used to have this rabbi that reminded me of a Baptist preacher when he started the sermon—he would rant and rave and pound the pulpit to get his points across. And when it came time for the sermon, my father would reach up and you would hear "click click" as he turned off both those hearing-aid switches, and he would just sit there with the prettiest smile on his face and his eyes closed, and pretty soon he'd start snoring. [Laughs] And I can see that just like it was yesterday.

I can see the handwriting on the wall. Eventually this is gonna fall the way of all the other little synagogues and temples in the state. I can take you to Canton, Mississippi, right now and show you where they had a fine temple. The only thing left, it looks like a gravestone—it says, "This marks the spot of Temple so-and-so." And that's what it is—a gravestone for a congregation. And eventually, I think that's what we're gonna have. One of the younger members, younger than I am, he and I have a saying every time we go to a funeral for one of the olders: "Last one out, please close the gate." . . . I don't know, that's just the expression he and I use. "Last one out, close the gates." ■

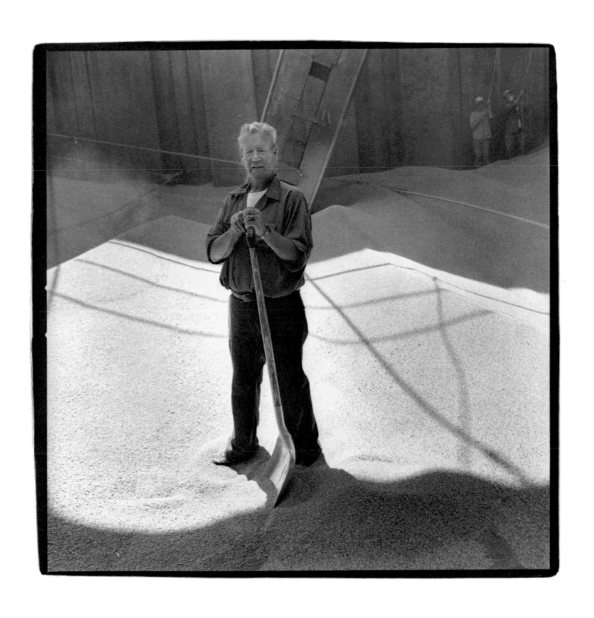

James "Jim Boy" Smith
GRAIN SCOOPER
BUFFALO, NEW YORK

We spoke with Jim Smith on the deck of a grain freighter just in from Duluth, Minnesota, while on break from scooping grain one August afternoon in 1993.

Grain scoopers have a long, rugged history in Buffalo's old First Ward. There was a time when this Irish-dominated trade kept more than a thousand men at work on the city's waterfront, scooping grain off ships and into silos for processing and shipment up and down the East Coast. That was when Buffalo was the nation's grain capital, the eastern terminus for all grain shipped from the Midwest.

But with the completion of the St. Lawrence Seaway in 1959, connecting the Great Lakes with the Atlantic Ocean, Buffalo lost its prominence as a grain center. Midwestern freighters were now able to bypass the city and sail directly into whatever East Coast port they chose. Almost all of the grain scooping at these newer ports was mechanized, and grain scoopers began to disappear. Today less than a hundred of them remain.

The grain scooper's task is to empty cavernous ships' holds filled with hundreds of thousands of bushels of grain. The scoopers use huge steel power shovels which slide on a pulley system to move the grain toward a conveyer belt (called a "leg") in one corner of the hold, which lifts the grain up into silos. When the hold is almost empty, the men scoop the last of the grain onto the conveyer belt with hand shovels.

Jim Smith was about to turn sixty-two years old when we met him. He'd been scooping grain for nearly forty years.

My name is Jim "Jim Boy" Smith—that's the nickname that the old Irish gave me years ago when I was a young kid, and it stuck with me. We all had different nicknames—"Diapers" Riordan, "Church" McMahon, "Bummy" Lawless, "Weepers" Cavanaugh, "Sleepy Hollow" O'Brien—everybody had one! They gave me "Jim Boy." If you called me Jim Smith today, I probably wouldn't answer.

I started scooping grain when most of the Irish were from the old country. I don't know how much you know about the Irish, but they're a little bit clannish, you know. They spoke with a brogue and they'd say, "Who's your father?" and "Who gave you your union book?" and "What county are you from?" They'd go right down the Irish tree. The union books were handed down from family to family, see? If the father was a scooper and he had a son, why he gave him the union book. I asked once, "If we're all Irish, how come we've got a few of these

Polish scoopers?" Well, if the scooper had a daughter and she married a Polish, they'd give the book to the son-in-law so there'd be vittles on the table.

I married a girl, her name was O'Leary. Her father gave me my union book, and he was from the old country too. Old harp from Ireland. Grain scooper. But I'll tell ya' he wouldn't tell me much. [Laughs] When I first started, I'd call the boss on the telephone for orders, and the man would tell me like, "Go to the Wheeler," which was a nickname for a certain elevator. So I said to my father-in-law, "Where's the Wheeler?" And he said, "Find your own way. I found mine and I come in this country with a full set a' clothes, and you came bare-assed!" They wouldn't help ya' a bit. They made you find your own way.

The old harps—the old-timers from Ireland, they called us "narrow backs," see, because we were born in this country and they didn't think we were strong

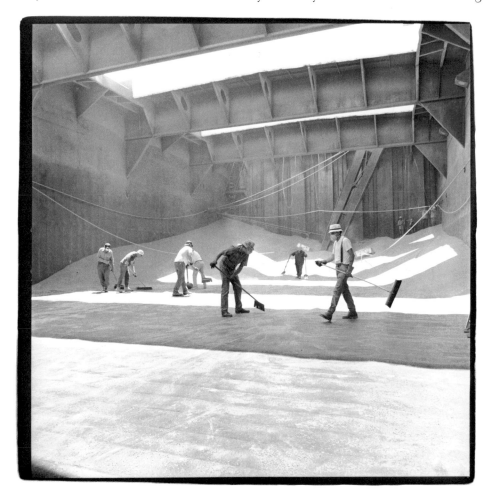

enough to do this. Years ago they had big iron shovels, and they were so proud they wouldn't let you touch 'em. They were maybe four hundred pounds, and one man'd work 'em. When we went to lighter stuff—like aluminum—the old guys didn't like that. They always told us, "Oh, it'll never work!" But it worked. When I had twenty years on the job they still called me a baby, 'cause some of those old harps stayed till eighty years old!

In the old days, if you were a grain scooper, why everybody loved ya, 'cause ya spent a good dollar in a tavern. In those days a lot of guys were "on the book"— you know what I mean? They'd put you on the book for your money and you'd come in there on payday and pay up. Every payday they'd be waitin' for you. You could get a steak sandwich for a quarter and a shot for a quarter, and the bar- tender'd say: "Have the first drink on me!" And you'd stay for a while—you could flop in the back if you wanted—take a sleep ('course the wives didn't like it much). There was many a fight in the taverns, many a Donnybrook. [Laughs] Years ago there wasn't much else to do. Wasn't any television. They'd play pinochle and poker, and they'd be arguing and they'd start calling each other names, then they'd go fight (the Irish are wonderful people, but they're famous for that). But there was never any hate—two days later they'd be back at the tav- ern drinkin' again.

People who come by and see us work say, "Oh my God, it's so dangerous!" And it is dangerous—people have gotten hurt. In the old days you'd get hit, but ya' didn't report it because you were proud. You might as well not tell it anyway, because they wouldn't give ya' any mercy. The boss'd say, "If you don't want the job, go home." They had their own way.

I have an aunt, she's eighty-nine but she's got a great old memory, and we still talk about it, the days of the scoopers—how friendly they were, how you could go to their houses and the door was always open. They'd have a beer for you and a cigar, and you could sit down and eat. That was how the grain scooper lived. Looking back, I'm just happy that I was one and that God was good to me. You finished with me? ■

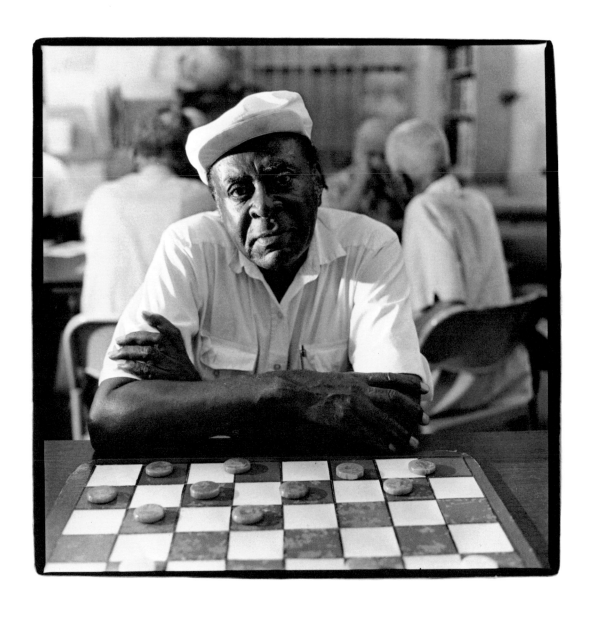

Jim Searles
PRESIDENT, BROOKLYN ELITE CHECKER CLUB
BROOKLYN, NY

Bulldog, The Mighty Claw, Pin Head, Pancho, Jersey Lee—some of the nicknames of the dozen or so men who gather every Friday night and Saturday in the library of a Salvation Army in downtown Brooklyn to play checkers. They sit at oversized green-and-white checkerboards spread out over two tables. The game is "pool check-ers," a more involved and fast-paced version of what many think of as checkers (the players call that game "straight checkers"). At one table, Clarence "Tijuana" Holt (a.k.a. the Clown Prince of Checkers) slams his pieces up and down the board in the match with a man they call the Mighty Claw, while at the next table Brooklyn Elite president Jim "Step" Searles and his vice-president, Charlie "Ghost" Free, are locked in a quieter but no less intense checker duel.

The game engenders an uncommon devotion from its players. Case in point: the Brooklyn Elites. The club started in the early 1970s to give pool checker aficiona-dos who had long congregated in parks, barbershops, and alleys a home base at which to play. A group of men, led by Jim Searles, rented a storefront on Fulton Street in Bedford-Stuyvesant and drafted their constitution:

Article II: Objectives
1: To promote the art and science of checkers.
2: To encourage those who play, study, teach, or write about checkers; all for the progress of checkers throughout the world.
3: To improve the image of the game, and to elevate checkers to a level of respect equal to or greater than that of any other national or international pastime. . . .

With that, the Brooklyn Elite Checker Club was born.

The past three decades have dealt the Brooklyn Elites their fair share of ups and downs. Yes, there have been the countless action-packed checker marathons stretch-ing from one night to the next (and sometimes longer). But there have also been set-backs, most notably that fateful day in August 1986 when a construction crew acci-dentally demolished the Brooklyn Elite's Bedford-Stuyvesant headquarters. They've been playing at the Salvation Army ever since, and dream of one day estab-lishing another permanent home for the club.

I first met the Brooklyn Elite's president and founder, Jim Searles, in May 1990. Jim's lived a most remarkable life. While working as a bellhop and longshoreman, Jim's passion for politics and the law always seemed to land him in the middle of historic events. He was at the Audubon Ballroom the night Malcolm X was mur-dered. He's sat in on just about every important East-Coast trial of the past sixty years—from Bruno Hauptmann's Lindbergh kidnapping case straight though the

Larry Davis cop-killing trial. "I always dreamed of being a lawyer but I never had money enough to go to school and learn it," he told me. "So all my life I always went to court cases, and I'd make my own notes and learn for myself." Politics, the law, and checkers. Jim is one of the wisest men I have ever known.

———————————

I started playing pool checkers during the Depression, way back in the thirties. At that time they called it "Spanish pool checkers." It was a good pasttime with nowhere to go to work. I faintly remember the first time I played the game was in a park in Philadelphia—that's where I grew up. Naturally, I lost the first time, and I got beat so bad that I just couldn't give it up. But I got better as I went along, and when I got on the WPA I just kept playing all the time—shovel some dirt, and then move some checkers.

After that I worked as a bellhop at the Douglas Hotel in Philadelphia. We had a checkerboard in the lobby, and boy, I played a lot of people. I played against most everybody in Duke Ellington's band—they was all crazy about checkers. They loved the game, but none of them could beat me. I got a kick out of playing Moms Mabley—that was Jackie Mabley. I played her, and I did learn how to beat her, even though she said I took too long to move. I played some games with Count Basie—we had a lot of fun. Only one who I could not beat was Jo Jones that played the drum for Count Basie's Orchestra. He could *play.*

We play pool checkers. It's a game that's played on sixty-four squares, twelve men on each side, black and white pieces—just the same as straight checkers, except for the method of jumping. In straight checkers you can only jump backwards with a king, you can't jump backwards with a single piece. In pool checkers you can jump forward and backwards with a single piece. Also, a king in pool checkers can go diagonally from one side of the board all the way to the other, as long as there's empty spaces to jump to. In straight checkers a king can only jump one square at a time. Those are the differences.

The history of the game has been a mystery to a lot of us. Some of the historians among us have found that the African-Americans played it during slavery times down in Louisiana. They was playing the same rules that we play—we found that out. The oddity of it was the whites down there played straight checkers. I'm wondering why the blacks didn't adapt themselves to the so-called masters—I think they wanted to be different. So still today in America you find the whites playing straight checkers, and the blacks, at least ninety-five percent, playing pool checkers. And then when you go to travelin', like if you're a soldier, you find out that they play the same as we play in Eastern Europe, the Soviet Union, and also in Holland. Checkers in Holland is like baseball here!

For many years, the mecca of checkers was a place called Mount Morris Park in Harlem—it's now known as Garvey Park. Our greatest player was Clyde "King Row" Black, and players from all over the country would come to New York to play King Row in Mount Morris Park, and they played all night. The great Carl "Buster" Smith—who was the American champion for many years—undefeated!—he'd come every summer to play. It was a great attraction. Another mecca for checkers was the barbershop. And if it was too hot in the barbershop or the barbershop close, then they play outside under the light. They play that way all night! You must understand, people get hooked on the checkers—they just play and play and play.

Well, I wasn't so happy with that kind of a life. I used to tell the guys, "You guys should be ashamed that we don't have a place to play!" So in September of 1972, I organized the club. I went around and found a man who would rent a place for one hundred and twenty-five dollars a month, and it was such a novelty that people joined right away—fifteen dollars to join and only five dollars a month. Man, before I knew it, I had one hundred and twenty-five dollars, so we got the place.

The first club was on Fulton Street. We must have had twenty-five or thirty

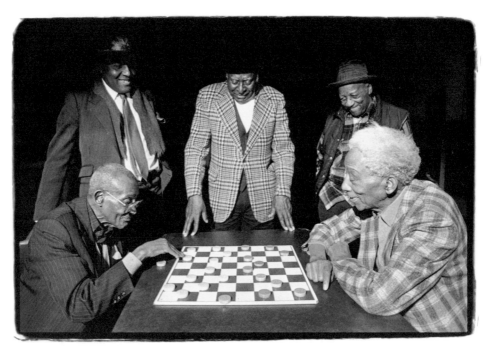

guys. It was just a storefront, and we played there for a couple of years until the rent went up so high we couldn't stay. Then we found another place right down the street. We decided to buy that building. They let us have it for five thousand dollars.

The guys kept it clean. It was comfortable. To tell the truth, we put in more time at the club than we did at home. That *was* our home. We didn't do nothing but play checkers. Most of the guys don't smoke and they not drinking people, so we just talk and play and talk. And like I tell the wives when they call and say, "Is so-and-so there?" I say, "No, he just went out to the store." She says, "Man, I'm gettin' sick and tired of him putting in all this time at the club. All he do is play!" I say, "Look, Miss so-and-so, if you got a husband playing checkers you got nothing to worry about—he ain't runnin' around with no women, he ain't messin' round with no liquor, he's just playing checkers!" [Laughs] I know some fellas whose wives get so mad they wind up throwing out their checker books (we all have checker books so we can study). I know one man who quit his wife because she threw out his checker books! My wife got used to it, man. Do you know that I missed my honeymoon because of checkers? [Laughs] Man, I'm telling you— it's a good thing my wife puts up with me. Nobody would believe it! One time we even had undercover cops come to the club, I guess to make sure we ain't got no drugs and no whiskey. After a while one of the guys showed me his badge. They couldn't understand what we were doing, going in and out at three, four o'clock in the morning. But they find out we wasn't doing nothing but playing checkers! They even shook our hands and said, "Man, you clean." Checkers gets in your system—that's all you want to do!

The pitiful thing about it, there was a building next to us that was unlivable. Well, the city paid to demolish it and the demolition people made the error of demolishing our building! That was five or six years ago, and we was very hurt because we had no place to go. The guys said, "What we gonna do?" We could go to the park, but not in the wintertime. We tried to go to each other's house to play, but that didn't work. We didn't know what to do with ourselves! So then one night I had this dream that a couple of guys up in Harlem told me to talk to the Salvation Army about playing there. I woke up that morning and said, "Listen here—I'm gonna see about this. They always helping people, so why not help us?" Well, I went to the Salvation Army, and talked to the man, the captain (I often wonder why they have military names like "captain," "lieutenant," and "major," but they religious people and seem to be living good). Well, the captain gave me the library where we could play—and it didn't cost any money. The guys were tickled to death when I found the place. Excellent place it is, and glad to have us here!

Checker players is really a brotherhood—like family. If there's a sickness in one of the guy's family, we raise money. If a guy gets unemployed, another guy will pay his dues. We look out for each other. I don't know no other group of people who do that. Other games you see people get up and fight each other in disagreement. The only way we fight is on that board. Our motto is "Win Like a Champion, Loose Like a Gentleman." We insist on that. Sometimes the guys get a little disturbed when they lose, but they only mad at themselves for making a foolish mistake. And if a new guy get out of line, we always remind him of the motto. That's something we all must live up to.

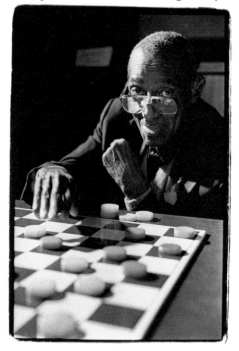

Jesse Calloway

It's a thinking man's game, see. A lot of people take it for a toy, like you buy a checkerboard in Woolworth's in the toy department, but it's not a toy. It's very, very complicated and a lot of concentration. It keeps me thinking. I don't think I'll ever become senile as long as I play checkers. None of the checker players, even the ones that's older than me, none of them is senile. Their minds is sharp. Like Jesse Calloway— he ninety-four and he's not senile at all. Only thing is he has that arthritis and can't get around, but his mind is good. That's all checkers!

Last year, when I went to see Calloway when he was in the hospital, I carried a board 'cause he wanted to play. He sit on the side of the bed in Harlem Hospital, and I play him five or six games of checkers. Why you think he don't quit? 'Cause he loves the game. A man don't quit what he love. Love is a great thing! ∎

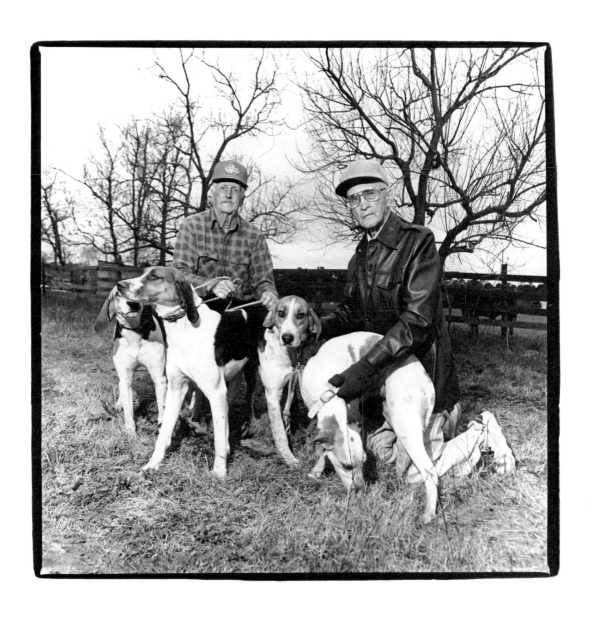

Hinkel Schillings and Shade Pate
Fox Hunters
Center, Texas

One of the finest nights I ever spent was under the stars with Hinkel Schillings (who was ninety years old at the time) and Shade Pate (Hinkel's nephew) on their week-ly fox hunt. It was November 1992 on the Texas-Louisiana border, and Hinkel and Shade were doing what they've been doing several times a week for more than sixty years—sitting around a fire from sunset until dawn, listening to their hounds bark. That's all there is to fox hunting—listening. There's no kill. A pack of hounds sim-ply chase a fox around and around in circles through the woods until the dogs get tired and return to their cages. The dogs bark all the while—the hunters call it "giv-ing mouth." The men know the voice of each of their hounds, and can tell from the bark how close each dog is to the fox. The hunters root for their favorite dog, remi-nisce about hounds of old, tell stories. But mostly they just sit quietly and absorb "the music of the chase." When a visitor's present, the men spend a great deal of time baying and yelping—imitating the barks of hounds past and present to illus-trate the finer points of the sport. On the night I spent with them, Hinkel and Shade ran about twenty hounds. I had a story to do somewhere else early the next day, and left the hunt at about two-thirty in the morning—missing the last act of the hound's symphony and the east Texas sunrise. I'll always regret that.

HINKEL: I'm Hinkel Schillings, and I was ninety years on the 11th day of this past April. I was born in 1902. When I was just a small little boy we had this neigh-bor that lived across the creek from my dad, and he had two foxhounds. I was too little to go but I remember how interested I was to hear about the fox hunting. Well, in due time I heard the hounds for myself. That was 1911. I was up all night long, so I guess I must have been a born lover of hounds, and still love it just as well as I ever did.

SHADE: I'm Shade Pate. I'll soon be seventy-seven years old, and I started hunt-ing whenever I was about fourteen years old. Had my first hound, old Joe Smith. He was an all-around hound. You can't make a hunter out of a man unless he was born one, and I reckon I was born one. My parents was hunters before me, and I've had hounds all down throughout the years. Yup. I've lost a good many hours' sleep hunting, but I've enjoyed every minute of it.

HINKEL: We've seen the sun come up lots of mornings a-huntin', and not slept a wink all night. Just listen. . . . There's all kind of voices: there's tenor, alto, bass, sopraner, and baritone. You take old Jim and Sam's got bass voices. You take

Smokey—he's got a baritone voice. You take old Cheater—he's got a tenor voice. Cover Girl has got a soprano voice. And you take . . . uhmmm . . .

SHADE: Snuffy, Lizzie . . .

HINKEL: Yeah. They've got alto voices, them high voices. It's a musical sound!

SHADE: Yup.

HINKEL: What a beautiful night that we've got—full moon. About thirty-two degrees. Still. The hounds are running hard all around about us. I want to tell you about a hound I had called Bone Hill Billy. He had distemper when he was a puppy, and that left him with a stiff hind leg that jerked. But when he went to runnin', he was outstanding! And he could tell you just how close he was to his game by the way he give his mouth. He started off just 'Yaw yaw . . . ooohhh ooh ooh ooh.' And then as he warmed up it was 'Ho ho ho . . . hoooo ho ho ho ho hoooo.' He'd thrill you to death! Now Shade, I want you to tell him about old Corene.

SHADE: She was one-eyed. When she was a puppy a cat scratched one of her eyes out. She'd run with her head in the air. Didn't have to put her nose to the

ground—she had a good nose! She run with a lot of different dogs and I never did see her get beat.

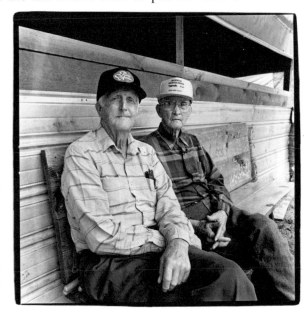

HINKEL: And a powerful hound she was! Now Shade, I want you to tell him about old Forty-seven. He was an outstanding hound that Shade had just a few years ago.

SHADE: Well, Forty-seven, he was a white dog. Beautiful dog. He had a big sage tail—that's long hair on his tail—and he'd run with that tail over his back, and his head up. He was the prettiest running dog. You see him coming across a moonlit night, his tail wavin' up over his back, and his head up. Looked like he was smiling! He looked like a picture! He had a big old heavy chop mouth, 'Yop yop yop yop yop yop yop.' You'd know him every time he barked.

HINKEL: If you got a good hound, and he's running with a pack of hounds, and you can tell that hound's voice, and your hound's in the lead, then's when you get the thrill! You can't help from hollerin' to save your life! You get so thrilled, that if you're subject to a heart attack, you might just near have a failure!

SHADE: Whenever you get out under the stars and a pack of hounds are running, you're relaxed, you are. You forget about all the worries and the turmoils that's taking place, and, well, you just feel closer to God.

HINKEL: You get a lot of lessons out a-huntin' under the stars, listening to your hounds. . . . It's wonderful.

SHADE: Yup.

HINKEL: Wonderful!

SHADE: Yup. ■

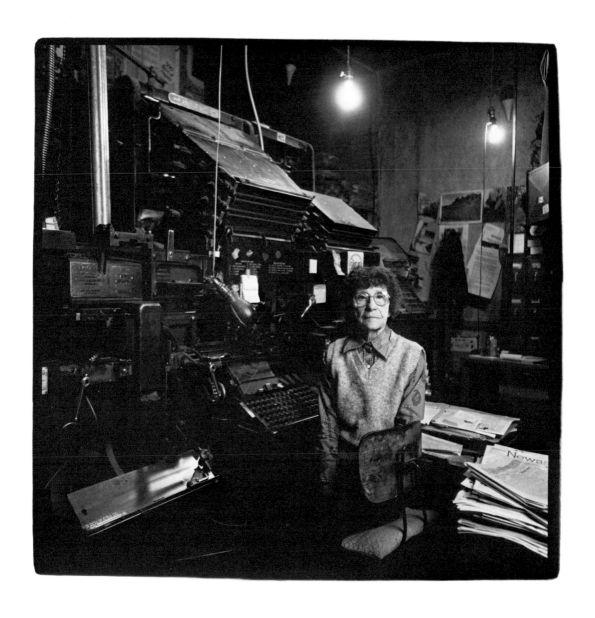

Marie Coombs
NEWSPAPER EDITOR
SAGUACHE, COLORADO

Marie Coombs started folding papers for her father's weekly, the *Saguache Crescent*, when she was four. At the age of sixteen she began setting type. She became the paper's editor at twenty-one. Today, at seventy-nine, Marie Coombs continues to edit the *Saguache Crescent*. And set type. And fold papers. Coombs works five days a week to put out the 114-year-old *Crescent*, one of the last "hot lead" papers in the country, with the help of her son Dean. "We don't have any reporters, we just do it ourselves," she told us. "It's mostly good news about people. We don't sensationalize too much. We like to put people's names in the paper, and if they come by to see us we try to write up a little something so they can see it in print. We have weddings and deaths and school news and church news. It's just four pages a week, but that seems to take care of it."

Coombs spends her days at the keyboard of the *Crescent*'s ancient Linotype machine, casting lines of type into molten lead. The lead-type columns are then laid out onto pages, locked into frames, and pressed. The paper comes out each Wednesday, a circulation of seven hundred in a town of seven hundred. "In all my years, we've never missed a deadline. Even when my husband died. That was the day after Christmas in '78. We had to do our New Year's edition. I told Dean, 'First we finish the paper, then we'll make the funeral arrangements. We can't take care of Daddy till after we get the paper out.' And that's what we did." ■

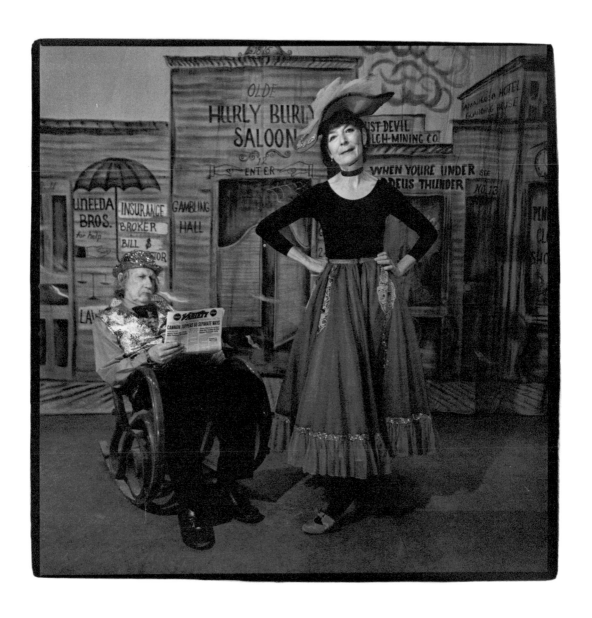

Marta Becket and Tom Willett
PERFORMERS, THE AMARGOSA OPERA HOUSE
DEATH VALLEY JUNCTION, CALIFORNIA

Marta Becket's dedication to her artistic vision is astounding. A frustrated New York City dancer, she happened upon the ghost town of Death Valley Junction, California, population 7, more than a quarter century ago. Since that time she's been putting on two or three performances a week in an old community center she cleaned up and renamed the Amargosa Opera House.

Her season runs from October through April, when the desert weather is somewhat less severe, and consists of half a dozen original shows Marta puts on with her partner, Tom Willett. Today she's become something of a Mojave Desert tourist attraction and sells out most performances. There was a time when she performed for no one at all.

I interviewed Marta and Tom inside the Amargosa Opera House late one night in August 1993. They were preparing for their upcoming season, rehearsing Marta's latest theatrical creation, On With The Show, *an "autobiographical retrospective of Marta's experiences in Death Valley Junction presented in song, story, mime, and dance."*

MARTA BECKET

Well, my name is Marta Becket and I'm from New York. Do you have to put my age in? Oh, horrible! Well, if you want to, put that I was born in 1924—I don't mind that. You know why? Because that's the same year this town was built. Now, to me there's something mystical about that.

Well, I knew I wanted to dance when I was three years old. I knew it. My mother would put records on the record player and I danced. She gave me the sleeves from her old evening dresses and chiffon scarves and I would dance constantly around the house, all the time making up dances. And theater—I was obsessed by it, and I played theater whenever I could. I loved being alone so I could play it, because kids my age didn't go for that—I was always kind of different. And my mother encouraged my artistic endeavors as long as it didn't cost her anything.

I loved Mother, but she had her faults. My mother never wanted me to leave her—everything was fine as long as I danced in her house. I never had any association with men or women, girls or boys—no, it must be *Mother*. It was hard, I suppose. Most ballet dancers I know are kind of coddled. They start when they're five or six years old and it's seen to that they have the proper training—they have lessons every week and they don't have the fear of having to go to work to support their parents. I had to support my mother—I had to leave high school and I had to dance in nightclubs and pretty tough places in my teens to support her. My mother had this addiction to the stock market. She took all the money I made and threw it in the market. She said. "This is for our old age, dear." As if I was the same age she was. [Laughs] She took all my money. And the reason I allowed her to do this is that my father married her best friend when I was about seven, and I thought that was a terrible thing.

Actually, working in the nightclubs wasn't too bad, because I'm a very creative person and I created my own dances that were all classically based—I did a Strauss waltz, a Czechoslovakian folk dance, a number in a tutu to Drigo's Serenade. Then the nightclub era died out, just like vaudeville, and there was no place to go and perform. So I got a job in the corps de ballet at Radio City Music Hall, and for two years I struggled there to conform and be like everybody else— thirty-one other girls—and it was very difficult.

After that I became disillusioned and completely gave up dancing for two years and began doing cartoons for fashion magazines, until I got a sort of you might say mystical experience at the end of that time. One night I was doing a cartoon. I was living with my mother and we only had one electrical outlet, so the light-bulb was hanging over my work and my mother was studying her stock market charts alongside me. All of a sudden I began to shake all over and I grabbed a piece of paper and started sketching something that I had no control over. It turned out to be a sketch of a dancer—a ballet dancer in repose. And in a very squeaky voice that didn't sound like me at all, I said to my mother, "I've got to get back into dancing! I've got to dance again, no matter how hard it is!" Her voice sounded like it came down a long corridor, and she said, "Oh, anything you want to do, dear, is all right with me." So, the next day I put on my old tights and bal-let shoes and started to exercise. I was determined to see this thing through.

I decided to take a chance, and I developed my own program of dance-pan-tomime and tried to tour and get bookings. I struggled and was hungry for about a year and a half. Then, finally, I got my first booking. That was September 1954. After that I got a three-week tour, then another three-week tour, then a twenty-week tour, and I was on my way. For nine years I toured as a solo dancer at schools and colleges and civic music associations all across the country. During this time I met my ex-husband Tom, who became my manager. I really thought I had made it. But then tastes started changing. By 1966, colleges were no longer booking performers like me. They were booking rock bands. The solo dancer was just fading out. And I was at my peak. It was very discouraging, but I wasn't about to give it up just because the wind blew in a different direction.

We had a vacation in 1967 during Easter week, and we camped in Death Valley—this was a very down period in both my ex-husband's and my life. We got a flat tire and were told that the best place to have it fixed was at Death Valley Junction. So we came here and had air put in the tire. When that was being done, I happened to look around and I thought to myself, "My God, this is a wonderful place!" Then my eyes rested on this building here. It was completely locked up, paint peeling—it was a mess! So while air was being put in the tire, I came around the building and looked through the hole in this door over here. I saw sunbeams shining in on various points inside. There was dust everywhere and an old calico curtain hanging up on the stage. There was a doll's head lying on the floor staring back at me right in the sunbeam. There was a magic to it, and I thought to myself: "This theater has got to be mine!"

I told my husband about it. We decided in half an hour to find the town manager and lease this building. The town manager was a character called Ariel—part of a religious group that lived here. He says, "What kind of shows you want to give here?" And we said, "Classical ballet and pantomime." Well, he didn't know what that was, but he said, "It's all right with me. You can have it for forty-five dollars a month, but make your own repairs." So Tom, my husband, built the stage. The roof leaked like a sieve, so he kept pounding tar paper on it over and over again—nothing seemed to work. But we decided we were going to open on February the 10th, 1968, whether it was ready or not. So I rehearsed every day, and that's when performances started.

Opening night we only had six wooden benches in the theater. Twelve people came—local people in their work clothes, children in their nightshirts. They really enjoyed the show—they understood what I conveyed because of the pantomime. That first season, sometimes we'd have an audience of two, sometimes nobody showed up. But I was not discouraged and my ex-husband was not discouraged.

That following July I looked up at the blank white walls in the Opera House and realized I wanted to paint an audience on them. It took me six years to paint these murals. They were very happy years, and also in a way sad years (I was going through a rather unhappy marriage, but I won't go into that). But in the happy times I would paint 'till four or five in the morning. The cool air of the evening would be coming in, and all the cats in the town would be draped on my scaffold as I painted. I was living in the Renaissance, and on the walls I painted balconies and a Renaissance audience from 16th Century Spain. You can see I have two balconies of gypsies there. I painted a king and queen on the top balcony, surrounded by nobility and clerics. The center is divided by a pair of double doors—there's a lady on one door playing a lute, and one on the other playing a tambourine. I have what I call the 'ecclesiastical' sections in the corners—the nuns on one side, the monks on the other (I couldn't resist putting them in). Then right next to the nuns I have on the top balconies the ladies of the night. And I became very aware of the ladies of the night because moving out here I discovered I was seven miles west of a bordello, and the Madame used to bring girls here every month for culture.

This is where I want to be. It's mystical, really. I feel as if I am meant to be here. I feel as if my life before this was a preparation for here. I've never felt like this anywhere else. I've lived long enough to realize that, for me, this is the best possible world. Where else could I do what I do? I've had a lot of disappointments in my life, but when I come in here it's my *sanctuary*—where I've made my life, where my creativity has been able to flourish. The world isn't very pretty out there, so I guess I made my own world in here.

When Tom Willett came to live here in 1982, it was a time when I was having very painful times with my husband. Tom came here to do the maintenance work. He used to pick up a broom and dance with it, and he did so many funny things around town that I thought, "Gosh, if that guy could do some of these things up on stage we'd really have something!" It wasn't soon after that I saw that my husband was going to have to leave. He went in January 1983 on the first night that Tom Willett performed with me.

Tom Willett

I met Marta about a month after she came here. I was working in a plant on the other side of Death Valley, and one day I came though here and I seen the sign out there that said, "Amargosa Opera House." Of course, just like everyone else, that boggled my brain—an opera house out here in the middle of nowhere? So, I stopped. Her husband at the time was standing outside, and I met him. This was in about August of '67. And over the years I kept up an acquaintance with Marta and her husband, Mr. Williams. Then in 1982, the plant I worked in closed down and everybody was laid off. They needed a maintenance man for the town, so I came over here to be a maintenance man—and wound up on the stage! [Laughs]

When I came over here to be a maintenance man, I was always doing these crazy antics. Like I'd ride my three-wheeler with my feet up on the handlebars, laying back and looking up at the sky and going [barks loudly] "Arf arf" all over town, and things like that. Well, Marta seen me doing all these things, and she thought it would be great if I could do it up on the stage. I told her, "It's one thing doing it out there, but it's another thing doing it up there on stage." But she decided to try me out. So she put together a number called "The Second Mortgage" that included me, and it went over great! From then on she has made a comic actor out of me! Marta and other people tell me—I can't brag about myself—that I'm a natural up there. It was a late calling, you might say. ■

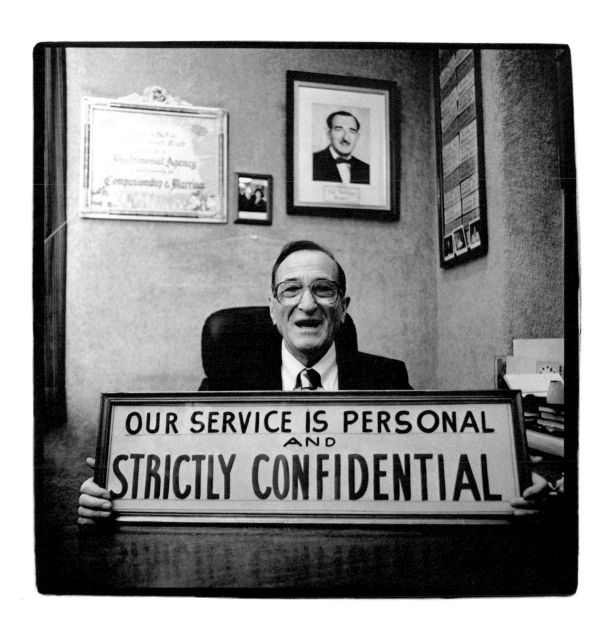

Dan Field
MARRIAGE BROKER
NEW YORK CITY

Brrring. "Hello, Field's? . . . Oh, you're a medical doctor? You like to meet a nice lady? Sure. . . ." And so goes life at Field's Exclusive Service in midtown Manhattan, run for more than seventy years by Dan Field and generations of Fields before him. "I work seven days a week, eighty hours a week. No gimmicks, no nothing—the real old-fashioned way!" Field explained when I met him in 1990. "I have more than eighty thousand people to choose from—from sixteen to eighty-five. I have all walks of life, all over the world. All religion, all race. I have poor ones, I have rich ones. I have high society, millionaires, models, actors, actresses. I have high class, I have medium. It's a department store in here. Whoever comes in here, they give me an order, I deliver!"

To the best of Dan Field's knowledge, this all started in Russia with Dan Field's grandfather, the Rabbi Joseph Field, who, it's said, had a knack for matchmaking. When the family immigrated to New York in 1917, Rabbi Field decided to turn his gift into a business: "Field's Exclusive Service," with the no-nonsense slogan "I Can Arrange." In 1930, Rabbi Field retired and passed the business on to Dan's uncle Irving Field (author of the matchmaking opus How to Marry and Find Love and Happiness). *Dan Field took over some thirty years ago. Since that time he has arranged thousands of marriages. "Who walks in here, they are ready and sincere!" Dan told me, his eyebrows twitching wildly. "They don't come here to play games! They're ready to make a commitment!"*

Okay. You could put the microphone down, and I'll hold it. I'll hold it. I'll hold it. You want to hold it? Okay, all right. My name is Dan Fields F-I-E-L-D-S [*sic*]. I am an old-fashioned matchmaker. I am the third generation in this business, making people happy all over the world—that's millions and millions of lonely people, which they cannot meet the right one and they don't know where to go to meet them, so they come to Field's and we make arrangements for them to meet the right one. And we have parents which they coming in here for they children that cannot meet the right one, so we make arrangements for the children *without their knowledge.* But I don't tell them who to marry, who not to marry. They have to decide—but at least they gonna meet someone for a future through me!

They coming in here, they tell me what they want, what they're looking for, they fill out a card, I talk to them, they tell me all about themself: their age, the type they want. I send a list of names to them—five, six or seven, it doesn't matter, we have plenty on file. Then the gentleman calls up the lady to make a date to go out, and they meet each other like they lookin' for each other. Then it's up to them to decide. The chemistry has to be there. If the chemistry is there, fine. If no chemistry, we send them more and more and more—there's no shortage. At the end they give me a report. Nine out of ten they tell me, "This is the right one!" And they get happily married—that is the purpose.

If they come in here, they're not interested in living together. They're interested in living together *forever*—legitimately. I have parents that coming in here from all over the world. They write to me, or they come in here. They have daughters, they have sons. Sophisticated—doctors, lawyers. Highly educated! But they cannot meet the right one. If they do meet the right one, he doesn't want to get married, he wants to move in—you know that's the style, "moving in". So the parents don't like that—they want to see their children *happy*, like every parent. So they come in here for the children without their knowledge, and I make the arrangements for them. They meet the right one, they get happily married—*forever*! And they don't have to know anything about it!

I made thousands and thousands of matches—who could remember all of them? A young lady I married off one time. She was six-foot-two, one hundred and five pounds—a shoestring, you know—nothing here, nothing there. She had a Ph.D. degree—highly sophisticated young lady. "Mr. Fields [*sic*], I have a problem to meet the right one." I look her up and down, I say: "You sure do!" She says: "But I don't care how tall he is or how short he is." Then I have a man coming in—it happens all the time. He was about five-foot-eight. "I'm looking for a tall girl, I want to have tall children." I say, "What makes you say so they're going to be tall? Maybe the children will take after you?" I call her up: "I have a young man, highly educated, about five-eight or so. He likes a tall girl." "Sure!" I made arrangements. The first time, and that was the end of that. They have a child already now too.

I have men coming in here, "I want 'em this way, I want 'em that tall, I want a blonde, I want a this . . ." I say, "My friend, I'll put her in a mold, we'll take her out, and we'll give her to you. But you didn't ask the right *question*, my friend. You didn't say: "She should be a model *inside*. Outside people change, clothes you could always buy, neighborhoods you could always move, but you didn't say the *inside!*" The inside you cannot change. The outside could be changed. You have to convince them! ■

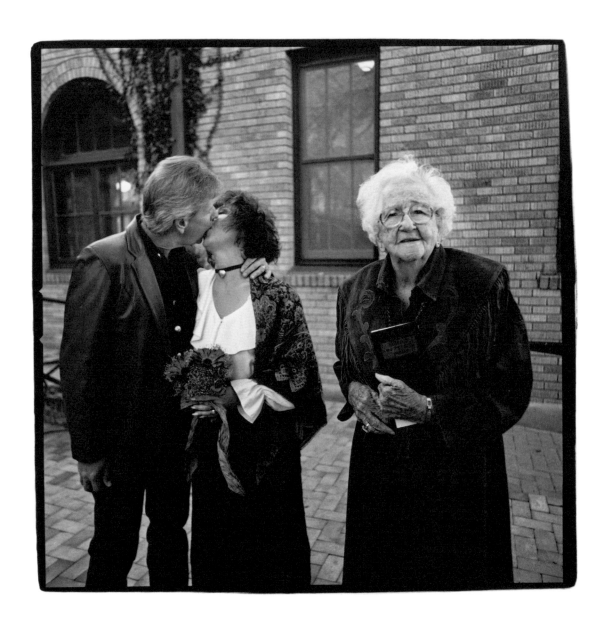

Hallie Stillwell (and newlyweds)
JUSTICE OF THE PEACE
MARATHON, TEXAS

We crossed paths with Hallie Stillwell one morning in November 1994 in Marathon, Texas, as she was preparing to join John Hoyt and Shelley Mesa in holy matrimony. Hallie had recently turned ninety-six years old. Although she had retired as justice of the peace for Brewster County (a swath of rugged southwest Texas land half the size of Connecticut) more than a decade earlier, Hallie was still called on to officiate at weddings nearly every weekend.

Hallie began her career in 1916, as a teacher in the border town of Presidio, conducting classes with a six-shooter tucked in her skirt (the Mexican Revolution was still in full swing). Two years later she married a cowboy named Roy Stillwell. Together they rode the range, herded cattle, and built up one of the most successful ranches in the area.

After Roy Stillwell's death in 1948, Hallie struggled successfully to hold on to the ranch (unheard of for a woman at the time), which she continues to run to this day. She also writes a weekly gossip column for the local *Alpine Avalanche* (she's had the column since the early 1920s), runs a dry goods store and RV park (with the help of her daughter Dadie), and officiates at weddings like this one. "I just hope they'll be happy," she said after the ceremony. "They'd better be!" ■

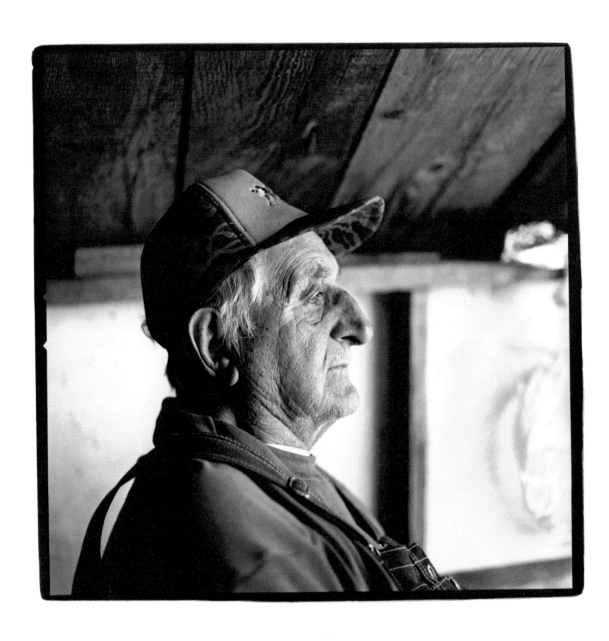

Percy Brigham
SCAFFOLD FISHERMAN
CASCADE LOCKS, OREGON

Every year, from June until early October, Percy Brigham lives by himself on a wooden platform jutting out over the Columbia River. Percy, a Walla Walla Indian ("We're so good they named us twice"), has been fishing the Columbia for more than sixty years. He's one of the last in an age-old tradition of Native American scaffold fishermen, thousands of whom once dipped their nets in the Columbia for salmon. The construction of hydroelectric dams in the thirties, forties, and fifties caused scaffold fishing to all but disappear from the river. It didn't stop Percy Brigham, who continues to fish at the age of eighty-four. "It's hard to give up," he says in his slow, husky voice. "I wouldn't know what 'take it easy' is anyway, goddammit! I want to live my life, I don't want to just lay around."

For at least five thousand years, Indians have caught salmon off wooden scaffolds on the Columbia River, most staking out a spot near a place called Celilo Falls (about sixty miles east of Portland), one of history's great fisheries and trading posts. Thousands of Indians once lived at Celilo, in lodges along the banks of the Columbia, and fished the swirling water flush with salmon at the top of falls. Indians called it Wy-am ("Echo of Falling water"), and each fall Native Americans from all over the Northwest would travel there to feast, trade, and pray. "Celilo was the greatest fishin' that the Indians ever knew," recalls Brigham, who started fishing the falls in 1930. "Years ago they'd spear 'em there, and a lot of times their spears would go through two fish at one time—I've seen 'em that thick! I've seen 'em awful thick there. At Celilo some days we'd take *fifty tons*, the Indians would. Several times I took in over a ton in a day *all by myself!* In the wintertime we'd go in debt, but then we'd go to Celilo in the spring, and in a week's time we'd pay up our debts. I'd see more fish in one day there than I see in a whole year now!"

The beginning of the end of platform fishing on the Columbia came in 1934, with the opening of the first major dam on the river, the Rock Island. In 1938 the Bonneville opened. In 1940 the Grand Coulee. While each of these dams wiped out ancient tribal fishing sites, Celilo Falls remained intact. In the early 1940s, the U.S. Army Corps of Engineers began working up plans for a hydroelectric dam at The Dalles, about eight miles downstream from Celilo. Despite vigorous protest from Indian groups, in 1950 Congress authorized the building of The Dalles Dam. Construction was almost complete when the government approached the tribes that owned Celilo's fishing rights for a settlement. "Instead of coming to us fishermen, they waited till we was all fishing and then come to the tribes so they wouldn't have no opposition," Percy Brigham remembers. "The agent said, 'We'll give everyone three thousand, seven hundred and fifty-five dollars. Well, Christ, all the people who didn't fish said, 'Sure!' So that's how they beat us out of Celilo."

On the morning of March 10, 1957, the massive gates of The Dalles Dam closed, arresting the surge of the Columbia. Six hours later, Celilo Falls was completely submerged. "People come up there to watch the water rise over Celilo, but I couldn't stand to watch it. I didn't want no part of it," Brigham says. "It was just sorrow—like if they put my mother away. I couldn't go by Celilo for ten years after that without it being just like I'd lost my best friend. That was my livelihood, and as far as I was concerned, that was the end of me."

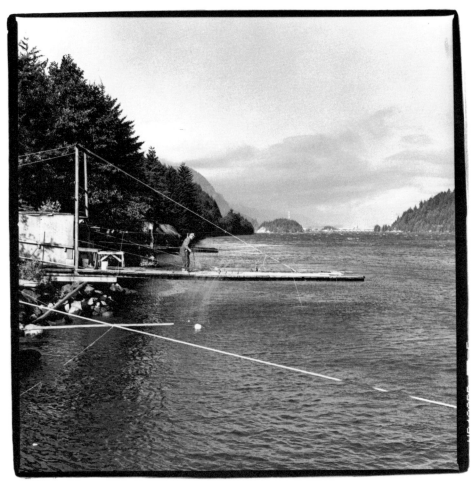

It wasn't. After the flooding of the Celilo, Percy Brigham regrouped. Before long he had switched from salmon fishing to sturgeon fishing, and had given up his platform for a small boat. For several years, Percy fished sturgeon up and down the Columbia with the help of his two sons and two stepsons. The boys branched out on their own. Today, the three oldest share a boat and fish sockeye salmon in Alaska. The youngest runs his own boat on the Columbia.

Percy, on the other hand, eventually returned to platform fishing. "I had bones broke off on the small of my back, and I had five ribs that broke free. I couldn't take the boat rocking around in rough water anymore, so I just went back to scaffold fishing altogether." He continues to this day. One of a handful of Native American scaffold fishermen remaining, Brigham lives in a tiny shack at the foot of his splintered platform for four months of the year. "I'm pretty well crippled up now," Percy says, rattling off some his ailments: two artificial knees, an artificial hip, bronchitis, and prostate cancer. "I don't know why I don't give it up. It's just in my blood. I guess." ▦

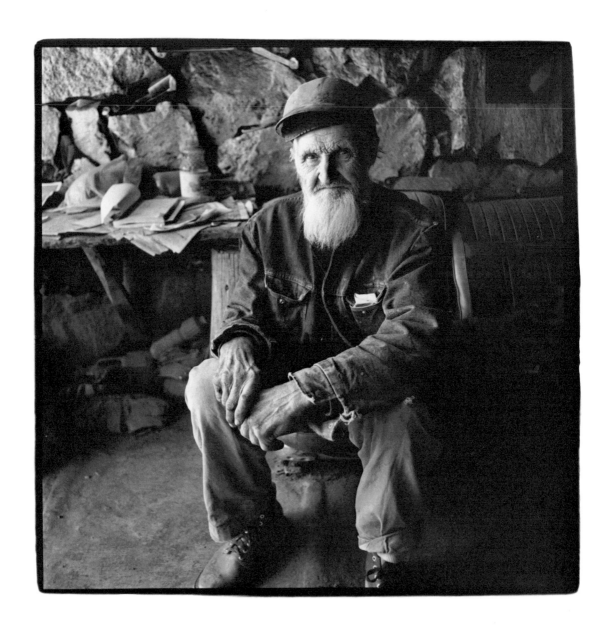

Dugout Dick Zimmerman
PROPRIETOR, THE DUGOUT RANCH
SOUTH OF SALMON, IDAHO

Harvey and I visited seventy-seven-year-old Dugout Dick Zimmerman at his complex of caves-for-rent in Idaho's Salmon River Mountains on a cold November day in 1993. Dugout is an original: a mountain man who settled in a remote Idaho cave, only to find his outpost of solitude become a magnet for others much like himself. "I started out as a hermit, but I'm in the tourist business now," Dick explains in a soft toothless slur, zigzagging up his mountain-cum-hotel, also known as the Dugout Ranch. "It's a pretty good deal if you want to rough it a little. I only charge two dollars a night for a room. No swimming pool, but we got a hot springs over that hill. No TV, but I play the guitar, and the people seem to like

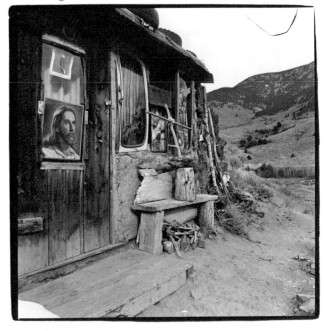

it." Taking his own cue, Dick straps on a guitar and launches into a lengthy and somewhat tuneless rendition of "Listen to the Mockingbird."

The Dugout Ranch sits about eighteen miles south of the town of Salmon, Idaho. From a distance, it looks like a series of abandoned mine shafts. Dick spends his days there, deep in a cave, lying on his stomach, pick in hand, mining for precious metal. This, he explains, is the process by which his hotel has come to be: first he picks a spot on the mountain which he deems likely to yield a deposit of silver or copper. Once he concludes his excavations, Dick converts the mine into a room, building and furnishing it with materials he's procured from a nearby junkyard. Dick seals off the entranceway to each cave with a facade of rock and mud. He installs a scrap-wood door and a large window made from an old car windshield.

The rooms are surprisingly pleasant, even cozy. Each has a wood-burning stove made from a trash can, and a box spring and mattress. The more deluxe rooms have an old school-bus seat for a couch, and an empty icebox in which to hang clothes. All the rooms offer a picture-postcard view of the Salmon River and the mountains beyond. The walls are made of stone with a layer of mud underneath ("to keep the mice and rats from digging through"). "It's cool in the summer and warm in the winter," Dick points out. "I've been here since '48. Wouldn't want to live nowhere else but a cave!"

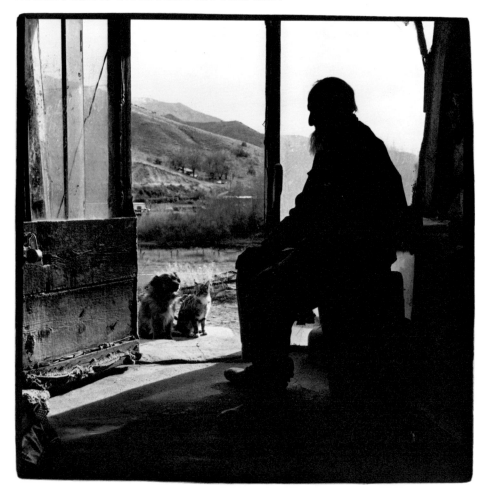

"I was born in Indiana. Run away from home when I was eighteen. I was in Nebraska for a couple of years, then I hitchhiked over here. When I saw this place I said, 'I'm moving in!' And that's what I done, just like that. Wanted to be by myself, but people started walking over here. They'd say, 'How much it cost you to live here?' Or 'How many more of these caves are you gonna make?' And then they give me a drink out of their bottle, and some of 'em give me a few dollars, so I said, 'Heck, I'm gonna start charging!' "

On the day we visited, guests occupied half of the ten caves Dick rents out. In one room a reclusive elderly woman, in another a hitchhiker from San Diego. "There are some things I don't like about this place and some things I do," says Dan, the grizzly-voiced occupant of cave #1. "I don't like the dust. I do like the solitude, the reclusiveness. I'm away from town. Bars. Out here I have to become introverted, and that's a scary damn deal—looking at yourself. Really scary."

"It's just a bunch of rocks without him," adds Joe, another ranch resident, pointing at Dick. "It gets sort of awkward trying to describe the idea of living in a cave in Idaho, but for some people it makes a lot of sense." ■

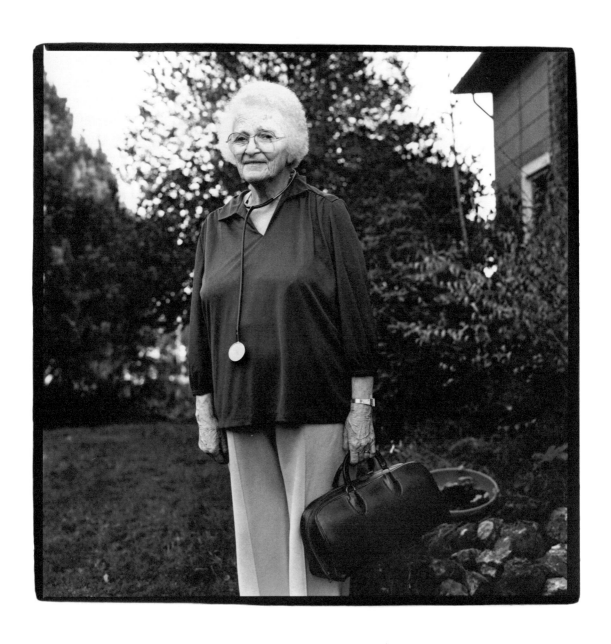

Lydia Emery
COUNTRY DOCTOR
YONCALLA, OREGON

We interviewed Dr. Lydia Emery in the kitchen of her cottage, which doubles as her office, in the mill town of Yoncalla (population eight hundred) about fifty miles south of Eugene. For nearly fifty years, Emery has been the town's lone doctor, dealing with everything from earaches to mill accidents. When we met her in 1993, she'd just turned eighty-four years old, and was still charging her 1940s fees: one dollar for an office visit, two dollars for a house call.

I grew up in Iowa. Johnson County. My people, they didn't believe much in education, and for a girl even to go to high school—I had to wait three years for that. We lived on a farm, and there were no school buses to take you there, so it was the goodness of my father that he decided I could live in town and go to high school. After high school I taught in a little one-room schoolhouse for five years, and then I went to a Mennonite college.

My younger brother, I don't know where he got the idea, but I know he was not more than five years old when he said he was going to be a doctor when he got big. So somebody said to me, "Why don't you go into nursing?" And I said, "I'd much rather be a doctor." That was something that just came out of me—I had never even considered it. I heard myself saying that and I wondered, "Where did that come from?" Because you don't even *think* about something that far out.

Anyway, I took pre-med at university, and I applied for medical school. My father didn't know anything about it. At that time, I used to faint pretty easily—our whole family faints easily—and I was just afraid that if he said "no" I would fall to the floor. My folks were getting kind of old, and you want to shelter them from some of the hard facts of life, so I just didn't say anything. But one day, a man came to the house and wanted Dad's signature for something, and he said to my dad, "I don't know how you do it. Your kids all really know what they want. And now Lydia's going into medicine. . . ." And my father looked at me, that was the first he had ever heard of it, and he asked me: "Are you planning to go to medical school?" And I said, "Well, I applied, but not everybody that applies gets in, especially not girls." And he didn't say anything for a bit, and then he said, "Well, I guess you're as good as anybody." And that was all he ever said. And in the end he helped me borrow money for it and everything.

I graduated medical school in 1941, the year of Pearl Harbor, and went into the navy for two years. That's where I met my husband, Jeep. We came to Yoncalla in '46 so Jeep could find a job in the mill. There were a lot of people coming into town at that time for logging and the sawmill. I intended to set up a little office, but before I got around to it, people started coming to the house. They knew that I was mostly interested in youngsters, that I had taken a pediatric residency, so they mostly brought their children. But the adults came too.

At that time, an office call was around three to five dollars, but I didn't have any real setup of an office, so I just started charging a dollar. We were all starting out together, and I knew how it was, going from one paycheck to the next, so it wasn't anything unusual. But as the years went on, I just kept my original fees. I remember at one point, when the mills were doing well, I thought, "Maybe it's time to raise my fees." Then the plywood mill at Drain burned down, and I just forgot all about it. So I never raised my fees, and it's still the same today.

I have met people who think that if you could make a lot more money, you should. Like one of my own colleagues, a woman doctor up in the valley. I didn't know her, but one of my nurse friends told me that she was very upset with me because I didn't charge more, that I was "projecting the wrong image," that a woman doctor should make just as much as a man doctor—which I don't disagree with for one minute. But I was very upset by that, because to me, medicine should be a measure of what you're doing, not how much money you're making. You don't say, "I'll do a plain appendix sew-up on you and I'll make fancy stitches on somebody else!" I mean, medicine just isn't that kind of thing! The qualities like a sound basis of knowledge and good clinical judgment and diagnostic acuity and empathy and compassion—*that's* what medicine is about. And gender doesn't enter into that, and neither does money! ■

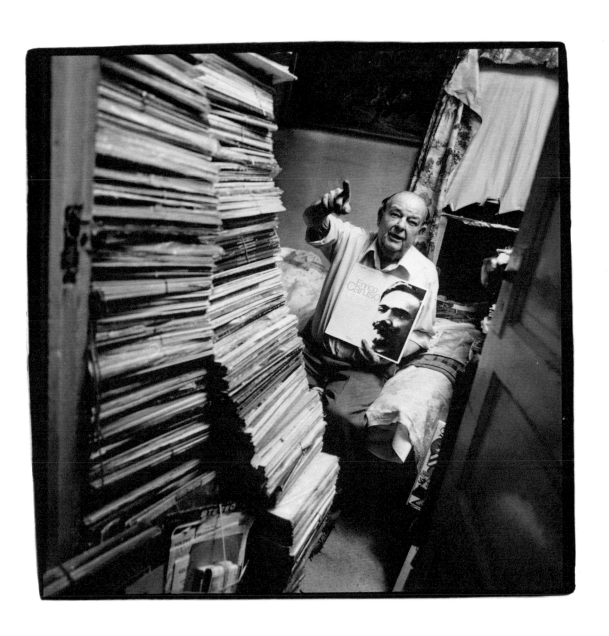

Stanley Kilarr
Record Collector
Klamath Falls, Oregon

One might suppose Stanley Kilarr's house is abandoned. It seems on the verge of collapse. The whole structure sags. The front door is boarded over. Its filthy windows are covered with rags. But inside, life! Stanley Kilarr, seventy-nine years old, hard at work organizing his record collection. More than ninety thousand 78s and LPs in all. One of the largest collections in the world. So much vinyl that his house is literally sinking under its weight.

"This is something, huh?" a somewhat disheveled Kilarr asks, showing us in. "But we got every record here that was ever recorded. The collection covers *everything,* from Edison's 1887 cylinders right up to about 1990."

Kilarr gives us a tour, winding us along the narrow channels he's carved between six-foot-high stacks of records. On his front porch, the oldies. In his bedroom, the orchestras and movie sound tracks. In his kitchen, the polkas and yodelers. In the bathroom, country and western. More than five hundred Gene Autry LPs in his tub. "This is important stuff. Real expensive!" he says. "Be careful now, don't fall!"

"First record I ever bought was seventy-five cents, and boy that was a lot of money in 1924! It was 'Yes, We Have No Bananas.' I was born in Portland, see, and on the street that I lived there was this Greek merchant, and he had a fruit stand. Well, he had a phonograph out there, the hand wind-up kind, and he used to play 'Yes, We Have No Bananas,' by two guys named Billy Jones and Ernie Hare, over and over and over. It just fascinated me! So I went out and found that *exact* record, and bought it, and that's how it all started. From then on, any voice I listened to that thrilled me, until I found it, why, I was never satisfied.

"A lot of people are like that. Many people write to me, elderly people, wanting to know if I have this exact record that they used to hear when they were maybe eight, ten years old on the farm, maybe eighty or a hundred years ago — and I do! A lady wrote to me about her husband. He was in the Spanish-American War, and she wanted to know if I had this one particular song he wanted to hear, sung by this one particular guy. And so I put five takes of it, back to back, on a tape for her. And this lady sent me a beautiful letter when her husband died and said he used to sit every morning for about an hour and just play that over and over. It's just like anything classic: in time it draws you back and you want to hear it again."

When we met Mr. Kilarr, he was in a good deal of pain from ulcers on his feet and legs. To make matters worse, his collection had recently suffered through a rather severe earthquake. "I see a lot of damage back there, a lot of records toppled over," he told us. "That's the way life is, I guess: the good, the bad, and the indifferent. And now the doctor tells me that I'm gonna have to throw in the towel and sell the collection, maybe have my legs amputated. Still, about a week ago, I buy Frank Sinatra at auction. Four of 'em." He shrugs, with an impish smile. "I guess it's like a drunkard, always wanting a drink." ■

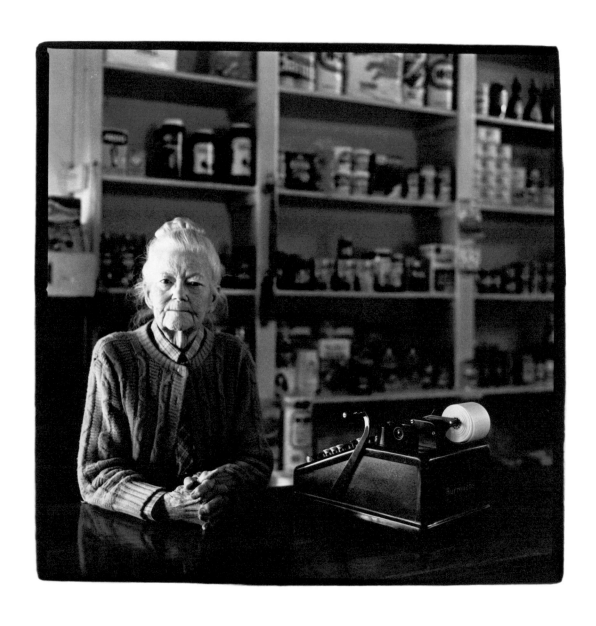

Marion Walker
CO-OWNER, HOWARD & WALKER'S GENERAL STORE
CANDELARIA, TEXAS

We found Marion Walker behind the counter of her general store in Candelaria (population thirty) on the Texas-Mexico border in November 1993. "This," she told us, "is the end of the world." Indeed, about thirty feet beyond her store the highway simply ends. It's the only business for sixty miles around.

Outside, an old gas pump which hasn't worked in years. Inside, high shelves partially stocked with produce beneath a pressed-tin ceiling and bare lightbulb. Marion Walker, a soft-spoken eighty-four-year-old, and her sister Nellie Howard started Howard & Walker's in 1948. "You come in the morning ready to wait on the people, you wait on them, and then you close," Marion explained, neatly summing up her career. "The years passed by so fast, we didn't know it." A few weeks before we arrived, Ms. Howard retired, leaving Marion Walker to run the store by herself. "Nellie just got tired, I guess." ■

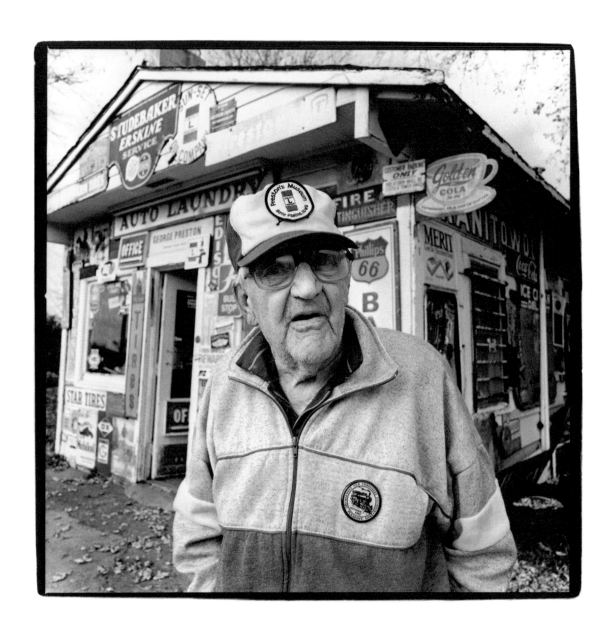

George Preston
OWNER, PRESTON'S FILLING STATION
BELLE PLAINE, IOWA

George Preston is an extremely excitable man. So excitable that when you meet him he's likely to dispense with the hellos and launch right into his nonstop Lincoln Highway monologue. George holds court from a beat-up rocking chair inside his filling station: the only station still in existence, he claims, to once sell gas on the country's first coast-to-coast paved road.

Started in 1913, the Lincoln Highway spanned 3,389 miles, from Times Square to San Francisco. It took a dozen years to pave the entire route, which was almost immediately swallowed up in the country's rapidly expanding network of roads. By 1927, the Lincoln Highway was no more. In Belle Plaine it was renamed Highway 30. George Preston would hear nothing of it.

George Preston's collection of Lincoln Highway memorabilia fills up his gas station and overflows into the garage next door. When he's not dozing in his chair, Preston spends the balance of his days talking to the curious who stop in to see what the filling station is all about.

This filling station was built in 1912, and this man run it. The man's name was Frank Feeney. One day I went up and asked him, "Would you like to sell your filling station?" He said, "What will you give us for it?" My father was with me, and I was thirteen years old. We said, "What would you want for it?" He said "I'd like one hundred and fifty dollars for it." My dad says, "I don't think it's worth it." So we started walking out and he stopped us and said "If you give me a hundred dollars, you can have it." We give him a hundred dollars for the station, and in three days we was in business down here on the Lincoln Highway. That was the 1st day of March, 1923—and I sold gas here for sixty-eight years.

I got over fifty thousand stories of the Lincoln Highway, that's what I got. There isn't a town on the Lincoln Highway from coast to coast that I can't tell you a story about it. And I'll tell you another thing, I got every kind of oil that was ever sold on the Lincoln Highway. One hundred and sixty-eight different kinds of oil—I got every bottle! The first oil that was ever sold on the Lincoln Highway was called "The Lincoln Highway Oil." From coast to coast there was forty-nine different brands of gas sold on the Lincoln Highway, and I got every one of *them*.

Do you know when I started this place I kept a list of every different kind of car that traveled the highway? There was two thousand, seven hundred and twenty different kind of cars that traveled the Lincoln Highway! There's eighty-seven different kinds of cigarettes that I sold in this place—and I got 'em all! Did you know years ago when I started in the business we nailed tires on cars? I'll show 'em to you before you leave! This is all Lincoln Highway stuff, and there isn't a man that comes in here that don't tell me that he can't believe it. And you haven't seen nothing yet! You're gonna stay a couple or three days with me, aren't ya? [Laughs] I had a guy stay with me a week here one time!

In those days, they had tent cities along the highways. Who ever heard of a motel? Now you probably don't know what a tent city is. Years ago when people traveled they took their tent with them, and they slept in their tents. And I run a tent city right here. We charged fifty cents a day for a family. Now, I'm gonna tell you a good one. One day a man pulled in here. He said, "Do you know where Vinton, Iowa, is at?" I said, "Yes. What are you going to do there?" He said, "We're going up there to work in the bean fields. Could we stay here?" I said, "Yeah, you could stay here." He said, "Okay, could we eat here?" I said, "Yeah." And one of 'em in his family said, "Bring out the milk!" They had two goats in their truck, and they took the goats out and milked 'em, and he said, "We always take our milk with us!" We had a little hydrant out there and he said, "Would you mind if I watered my goats?" And then they watered their goats! Well, the next day they went on into Vinton, and I haven't heard from them since. ■

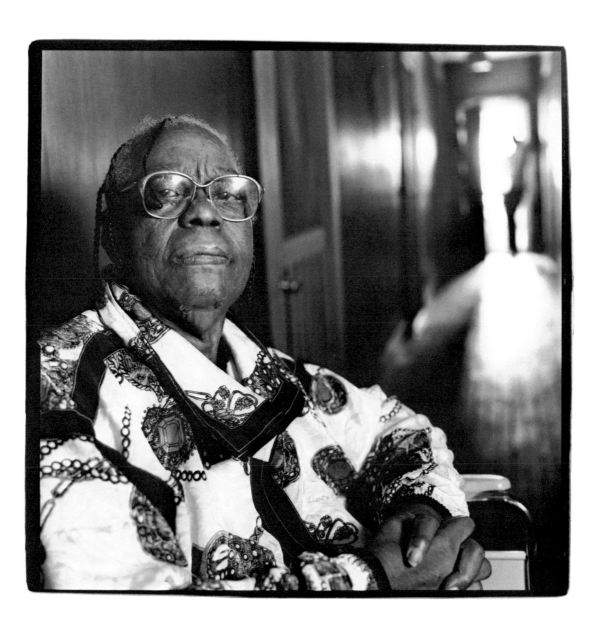

Z. L. Hill
OWNER, RIVERSIDE HOTEL
CLARKSDALE, MISSISSIPPI

The Riverside Hotel. There's nothing like it. Anywhere. Twenty rooms in a dilapidated single-story brick building. Peeling green stucco walls and shared bathrooms. But where else can you spend twenty five dollars to sleep in the very room Bessie Smith died in? Or sit in the parlor where Ike Turner and Jackie Brenston wrote "Rocket 88," which many consider to be the first-ever rock and roll song?

For fifty years the Riverside has lodged a who's who of music greats under the watchful eye of Z. L. "Mamma" Hill, who runs the establishment from a rocking chair in the front room (arthritis makes it difficult for her to move around too much). "You're at home now," she said, taking both of my hands when I showed up at the hotel in November 1991. "You want a can of soup? Go to my kitchen and warm it. Yes, you home now. Just bring up a chair and sit down. Now, are you comfortable? Let's talk."

I am Z. L. Hill. Eighty-five years old. Been here since November 9th, 1944, operating this building. Collecting the money, counting the money, keeping the books in the hotel. I used to live on Fourth Street—this street here is Sixth Street. Somebody came in one night, came and said, "Why don't you take that place G. T. Thomas got a hospital?" This was a hospital for colored only. I said, "Oh no!" He said, "The doctor's closed the place, and he's taking the furniture out." I called him. "Oh, Miss Hill, I'd be glad for you to take it. Come by in the morning." So we came down. I didn't like it when I saw. Didn't even like the location. But I took it.

When I first got here I didn't have no money (ain't got none now!) but I had faith. And the people came. Just drawn here. From all over. Everywhere! Because they knew when they get here I was gonna be nice to them. See, I do a lot of things for the people. If I have anything to eat, I give 'em part of my food. I have taken clothes off people and washed 'em in my washer and dried 'em, and have 'em ready for them the next mornin'! I tell them, "You can travel on now. Straighten out, go and take your shower, and travel on!" And you do that. Yes, you do that for people.

Everyone calls me Momma. "Momma! Momma! Momma!" If I sit on the front they be hollerin', "Hey, Momma!" I say, "Hey my sugars! Hey ya'll!" Yeah, all these boys that stay here is my sons. And do you know that this is a man's world in here? Don't no ladies live here—men only. It keeps down a lot of difficulty when you just have men only. It keeps down a lot of disturbance. Women like to fuss with the men, but if you get a bunch of men, they get along. Yes indeed, they are my boys. And all the band boys, when they lived here, they was my boys too.

Robert Nighthawk—he stayed here a long time. Blind Boys from Alabama, Joe May, C. L. Franklin—that's Aretha Franklin's father—all of them lived right here, had baths right here. And Sonny Boy Williamson from Helena, Arkansas, that blew the harp—he stayed right here with me. One night Sonny Boy come home from overseas, and I was sleeping, and he says to one of the boys, "I'm trying to find Miss Z.L."

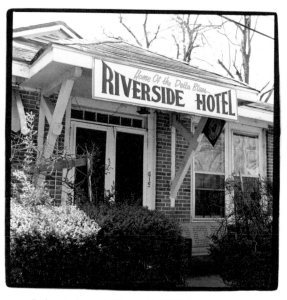

And the boy said, "She's worked all day, and she's sleep." He said, "Wake her up and tell her Sonny Boy's here! I want to talk to her!" I got up and he gave me his amplifier, and I hooked it up. He played that harp out on the lawn all night! And he drew a crowd—oh, he drew a crowd! He died a few days after that—wasn't over three days before he died.

And this is the place where Bessie Smith died. I used to see that lady. Every time she came to Clarksdale to sing the blues I was right there. Right there. She sang from a tent, big canvas tent with poles that raised it up. And they'd come in Sunday evening on the freight train, and they'd set that tent up, and they'd play the blues at twelve o'clock Monday afternoon up on Isaaquena to draw the people. Then on Monday night we'd dress fine as we could to go to the show and hear Bessie. She was the feature of the show. She waited until the last. You paid extra to hear her sing. And we sit there and listen to her sing, and she would sing and tell you about her man—her man is gone and he won't be back no more. "The Empty Bed Blues." And "Backwater Blues," when the high water was down in Greenville in 1927, '28, and people was all up in the trees hollerin', "Get me down! Get me down!" and the cows was swimming on the water.

They brought Bessie here from North 61 out of a car accident, because this was a hospital at that time. That room right there was the operating room. Room number two. That's where she passed. The room you staying in. Will you be upset? If you gonna be upset I'll move you to another room. So many people ask for that room! I don't know what's the idea, but they like that room for some reason. I had a man from Alabama and I had put him in room number ten and he said, "No, no! Put me in the room where Bessie Smith passed!" And then of course some of 'em wanna stay in the room where Ike Turner was.

I raised Ike Turner in room number seven down there. He came over here and got a room with me and I finished growin' him up right here in the hotel. "Rocket 88" you know about that? They put it together right 'cross that hall there. After they got that song together they went to Memphis to put it on record, and when they came on home that night, I said, "You all just might make it!" I made "Rocket 88" ties for they costume. Red ties. I embroidered R-O-C-K-E-T and then I put two eights across the bottom. And when they got where they was going, they looked good!

A lot of history been right here at the Riverside Hotel. But I'm just the caretaker, understand? The Riverside belong to the people. I tell you which way to go and what to do, but Bessie Smith made this their home. She died for this to be their home. Bessie Smith was the engineer, and I'm just ridin' on the train! ▪

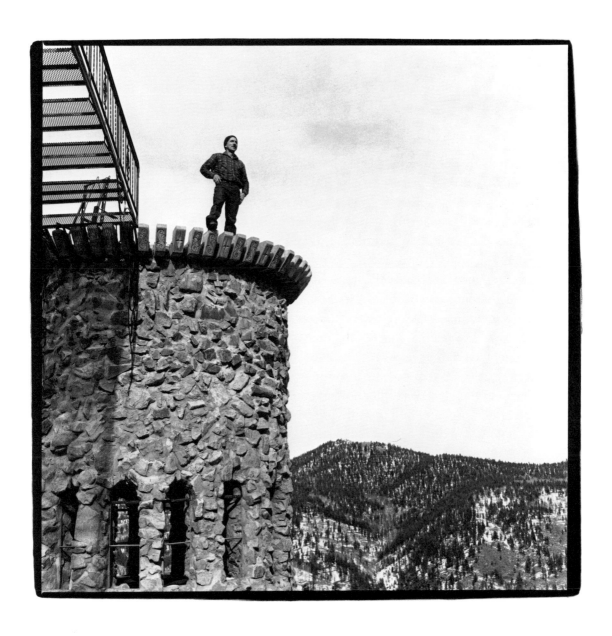

Jim Bishop
CASTLE BUILDER
NEAR RYE, COLORADO

Harvey and I showed up at Bishop's Castle one freezing November day in 1993 just as the sun was dipping below the hills. We found Jim Bishop hard at work on the project that's consumed him for the past quarter century: the construction of an elaborate medieval castle on a remote mountain in the Colorado Rockies.

Hello, there. Jim Bishop. I'm glad you guys are here, even though it's taken *twenty four years!* Well, this is it. Bishop's Castle. The world's biggest—with the help of God—one-man physical project, always open free to the public. A place of liberty, freedom, and justice. This is the poor man's Disneyland.

You want to walk in and look at it? It'll give you a better idea. I'm going to catch water off the roof, and pump it up to that corner tower. We'll have waterfalls, fountains, wishing wells. There'll be double wrought-iron gates here, and a wrought-iron-and-glass scenic elevator. There'll be a gravity-belt escalator down that far buttress—the weight of the people will turn automotive alternators, charging the batteries. You see the dragon at the apex of the roof? It's made out of discarded stainless-steel hospital trays. The lower jaw on that dragon is seven foot long. The two nostrils are a chimney. Someday it's gonna be a fire-breathing dragon. When the kids gather, I'll holler: "Turn that brass valve!" And when they do it will open up a full-pressure propane line, and a little electric starter will light it up, and the dragon will blow fire way out. Next year, I'll start start buildin' the walls around the castle, with a drawbridge and a big massive gatehouse. Doubt I'll live long enough to finish that.

When I was a kid, my dad spent all his time in our backyard, drinking. I'd sit out there with him, and look out at the hills, and think: "Now *that's* mysterious. I want to be in them mountains, see what them mountains are." So me and a neighbor friend started riding our bikes, and we would take off for the mountains. I loved 'em. Wild and mysterious. You'd always want to keep climbing to see what's over the other side. Well, there was this man from Texas, and he had this little two-and-a-half acre tip of land sticking into the woods. My folks didn't have any money, so I took four hundred and fifty dollars I had from mowing lawns, and I made a down payment on the property. I was fifteen years old. At that time it was all timber, and I started working: swinging an ax and digging roads. I went from a real shy, skinny and weak kid to exactly the opposite.

I didn't really like high school. Dropped out in the eleventh grade. I was in class one day and some cheerleaders come in and said: "We need a couple of volunteers to help us in the parking lot." They had these chickens in the trunk of a car as a stunt for a football game that they had dyed all kinds of colors—red, purple, blue, yellow. It was a hot day, and I go out there and open up this trunk, and here's all these chickens *suffering*. Boy, it made me madder 'en hell! So I grab the

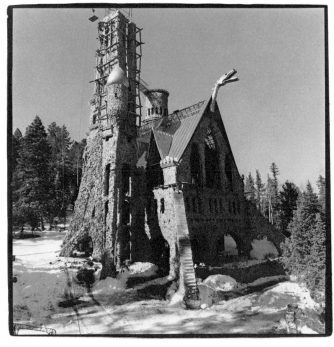

chickens and walked in school, and I says, "If that's what school's about, then I'm done!" So that's how come I quit school. The hell with that. I don't need that kind of crap. Them chickens got feelings too! Them chickens are children of God too! God created them chickens just like he created us!

A few years later I started building a stone cabin here, just to have a place in the mountains. My dad worked with me. He fell in love with the mountains too. Found out it was an even better place to drink beer. We started building, and people kept saying the rock work looked like a castle. That's how the idea of a castle come about, and I kept going. My dad argued with me. He couldn't see it as a castle, so he quit. He just wasn't a castle builder.

I just want to be recognized. . . . It's . . . It's *justice*. You ever hear of a guy named Buttafuoco? They go on and on about Buttafuoco. *What in the hell did he do?* [shouting] Did he do anything with his hands? Conan O'Brien. *Where in the hell did he come from?* Arthur Godfrey. *Was he an actor?* I mean, you hear about 'em over and over, and here you guys are, after *twenty-four years*, you're here! This has been newsworthy for *years*. I need this publicity. Not just me, the people need it. Do you know right now there's traffic on that interstate, and they're going to Buffallo Bill's Lookout Mountain Grave, they're going to see things in Denver and Colorado Springs. How many people are here? The three of us! It ain't any good unless somebody's here to see it! If somebody ain't gettin' any enjoyment out of it, then it's just a pile of rocks! ■

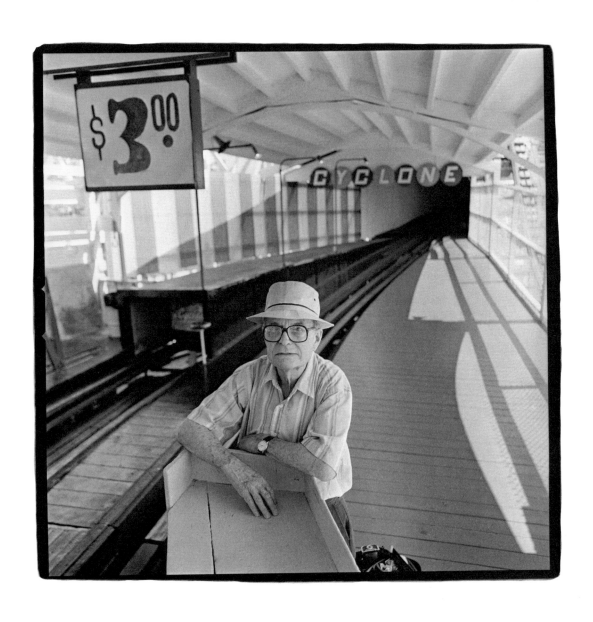

Matt Kennedy
DIRECTOR, CONEY ISLAND CHAMBER OF COMMERCE
BROOKLYN, NEW YORK

I first met Matt Kennedy in June 1990, when I was producing a feature that profiled three vestiges of old Coney Island: the maintenance man for the great Cyclone roller coaster, the owner of Coney Island's last remaining candy store, and two waiters (both named Sol) who'd worked at Nathan's Hot Dogs for forty years. I enlisted Matt Kennedy, who'd been with the Coney Island Chamber of Commerce since 1924, as my narrator.

Matt was a trouper. We wrote and recorded his narration in his small office on Surf Avenue, taking and retaking his lines as the subways rumbled past on the elevated tracks outside his window. It didn't phase him a bit. As president of Coney Island's Chamber of Commerce, Matt Kennedy knows a good challenge. In his lifetime he's seen Coney Island transformed from the world's pleasure palace, boasting three of the most spectacular amusement parks ever built (Steeplechase Park, Luna Park, and Dreamland), to a six-block strip of worn amusements in a crime-ridden neighborhood of poorly maintained housing developments and welfare hotels. "In my opinion," Matt insists, "Coney Island is still the most wonderful place in the world!"

Well, my name is Matthew Kennedy, and I've lived in Coney Island all my life. My grandfather was Italian. He came over from Genoa just prior to the Civil War, and he kept the lighthouse at Norton's Point at the very westerly tip of Coney Island during and after the Civil War. The light, of course, was turned by hand so it would face the channel at one time and the bay at another time. It was a twenty-four-hour-a-day job, and he practically lived on the beach. My mother was born in that lighthouse in the 1870s, and of course I was born in Coney Island in 1904.

My grandmother—she was born in Russia and came here to escape the czar— she was the proprietress of a tintype photo gallery in Dreamland. She lived over the photo gallery, and I used to stay with her a great deal. I was just a youngster, but I remember Dreamland quite vividly. I remember Lilliputia—that was a midget city where everything was miniature, and a colony of midgets lived there. I remember the Animal Show, Bostock's Animals. The lion tamer was a fella named Boniviture, and he had one arm—the other arm was torn off by the lions on a previous occasion. It certainly intrigued us to see him tame the lions and have them jump on pedestals and things of that nature. In fact I was at Dreamland about two weeks before the Dreamland fire in 1911. That's when this picture was taken—it was my seventh birthday. That's me in the center. It's a tintype. I remember the fire very vividly, because my father was the police lieutenant that sounded the alarm. I remember that Bostock's animals got loose, and they were running up and down Surf Avenue. They had to shoot two or three lions—they just ran rampant.

It was always a great day to go to Luna Park or Steeplechase. We got in there quite frequently because my father was the head of the police department, and we had passes. Luna Park had the old chute-the-chutes, where you went down a long incline in a boat and bounced into the lagoon. In the middle of the park they had a building that they set on fire, with people trapped in the third-story window (it was just fictional, of course). And they had the pavilion that depicted the Johnstown flood at Johnstown, Pennsylvania: it showed the dam burst, and the houses being swept away, all in miniature, in tremendous tanks twenty-five feet across. Then, of course, there was Steeplechase Park. You could go in there and buy a combination ticket with fifty rides on it for fifty cents. The main ride, of course, was the electric horses that went around the circumference of the park. Then on Surf Avenue they had the Coal Mine, which was a dark ride—the two-seater lovers'-lane type operation. We didn't go in that much, because we couldn't get the girls to go with us—they knew what they were in for! [Laughs]

At the present time, I'm the executive secretary of the Coney Island Chamber of Commerce. I've been associated with the chamber since its founding in 1924, but I didn't become the director until 1950. It's a one-man operation, and our job is to furnish tourist-type information to the general public throughout the country. Sometimes people call looking for lost relatives who used to live in Coney Island at the turn of the century. A lot of people call and want to know the temperature of the water. I have fun with some of them. I tell them to wait a minute and I'll go down and see. Then I go out and take a whiz, and come back and huff and puff—course I never go near the water—and tell them sixty degrees or seventy degrees—and they seem to be satisfied.

I still love the job, especially at this time of life. You'd be surprised how busy it is. 'Course, there's no comparison to the old days. Today, when people come down to Coney Island they see it through the eyes of a child. They don't see what we see—the empty lots and the neglect—they just see the lights and the rides and forget what's around them. I still have high hopes for Coney Island, though. There's an old tradition of those of us from around here. We say: "When you're born with sand in your shoes, it remains with you as long as you live." I guess I'll always have sand in my shoes. ■

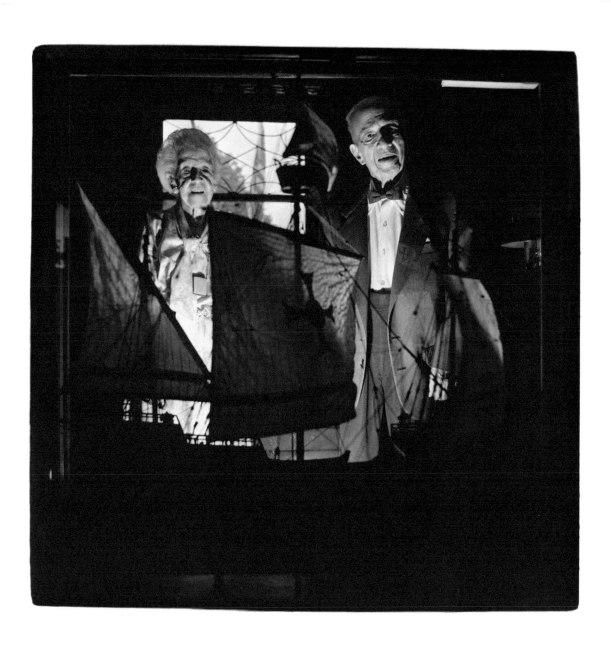

Mariano and Clara Lucca
CURATORS, THE CHRISTOPHER COLUMBUS AND QUEEN ISABEL MUSEUM
BUFFALO, NEW YORK

Harvey and I spent a memorable evening with Mariano and Clara Lucca in their museum / living room in August 1993. They are an intriguing pair. Clara, a quiet charmer, looks and acts a good deal younger than her ninety-seven years of age. Feisty Mariano, who talks endlessly, almost every sentence delivered in a raspy-voiced exclamation, is easily one of the more unforgettable characters we ran into over the course of this project.

MARIANO LUCCA: How are you? Nice to meet you. The pleasure's all mine. There's Mrs. Lucca there, always working. This is our museum here. The Christopher Columbus and Queen Isabel Museum. How do you like that ship there? The Smithsonian Institute offered *fifty-thousand dollars* for that, and here it is, sitting right here.

And that is the best statue of Christopher Columbus that has *ever been made*! And this is Queen Isabel, a *masterpiece*! She's going to be beatified by our Pope as a saint. She died in 1451. Do you know how many years that she's been waiting for her sainthood? *Centuries*, right? But the good Lord, my wife and I are going to be there as her sponsors, and she *will* be a saint!

My father's name was Francesco Lucca, and my dad was a great admirer of Columbus and Queen Isabel, because he felt that the queen was the one that made it possible for Columbus to make the voyage, and she was the forgotten woman of the discovery. At the turn of the century my dad had a saloon on Canal Street in Buffalo, and all of these men would sit in the basement, and they would plan about Columbus.

This was how I grew up. I grew up in having the fundamental principles. And I knew more about Columbus when I was nineteen years old than anyone who's writing a book today. College professors send me their books and I send them back and say "Correct this!" or "Correct that!" As a matter of fact, I got more here on Columbus than the Smithsonian Institute, and you can put that in spades! They wanted the copy of that picture there, I said, "Over my dead body." They wanted that ship, they didn't get the ship! That painting cost me nine thousand dollars, and the Smithsonian Institute wanted me to give it to 'em. I said, "No, sir!" They got nothing there!

Why don't you sit down here, Clara? My parental grandfather—my mother's father—told me, "Mariano, when you got married, you got to get a wife five years older than you because the man gets older five years faster." Well, it's the gospel truth. Here she is ninety-seven, I'm ninety-one, and we're just as even as we could be.

CLARA LUCCA: I'm gonna be ninety-eight pretty soon. We've been married *sixty-nine* years. . . .

MARIANO: Plus seven years of courtship. Don't forget that seven years! Those are the best seven years of our life, because that's what made Mariano Lucca *determined!* I saw her when I was seventeen years old, understand. *Seventeen years old.* . . .

CLARA: I was undecided if I should be a nun or get married. . . .

MARIANO: She said she was gonna be a nun. I said, "All right, I'll be a priest of your order." I'll tell you, that gave me *determination*, understand? By the way, this is the *original* painting of the landing of Columbus that the painter used to paint the same identical painting at the *Capitol*. Where would you find that? Everything we have here is all *authentated!* They call me Mr. Columbus, because I've been his great advocator. And I'm gonna make Queen Isabel a *saint!*

CLARA: A saint!

MARIANO: The Pope is going to make her a saint! And I'm gonna have her be Queen of the Americas. There's gonna be a national holiday in the United States for Queen Isabel! I'm gonna get that through Congress. I got enough votes to get that through Congress now. I'm the one that made Columbus Day a national holiday, understand? These are the pens here that President Johnson signed the bill.

At one time there was not so much agitation against Columbus, see? Now they say, "Columbus was a stinker." I says, [shouting] "You have a constitutional right to say what you want, but I got a constitutional right to tell you when in the hell you're *wrong!*" And we have made liars out of all of them—they're falling apart now. They say, "Lief Eriksson came over here first." Where did he land? I *liked* Lief Eriksson, understand? I tell you, when I was a young boy I had a great admiration for Columbus, but I *also* liked Lief Eriksson. In those days they used to have an oblong boiler to boil the clothes in—what they now put detergent in— the *washing machine*. Well, I took the cover of that as a shield. Then I took the colander that you drain the spaghetti in and put it on my head. Then I got a broom. And there I was: Lief Eriksson. I have *still* a great admiration of Lief Eriksson. *But he never hit the United States!*

These bums are nothing, see? And this museum will be here in 2092 fighting them all back on the goodness of Columbus. He is a saint in his own right, see? I talk to this statue of Columbus. I says to him: "Well, you got your day, and you're still gonna have champions after the good Lord calls us." Listen, it may be a statue, but there's a figure from heaven in there, understand? His lips open and he talks to me! And it isn't imagination of an optical illusion.

CLARA: Excuse me, may I say one word? We have a Columbus Day ceremony every October over here on the porch. It seems likes it's pouring rain every year, but it seems to me like when Mariano starts talking, the light starts to shine.

MARIANO: Queen Isabel stops the rain! A miracle!

CLARA: I got that in my scrapbook.

MARIANO: Listen. I want to tell you something. I got a great, great, great grandson that was born on Columbus Day! He was born when we were having our Columbus Day Banquet. I'm giving the awards. Well, I forgot all about the awards. I says "Ladies and Gentleman, I want you to know that I've been blessed of having a great, great, great grandson on Columbus Day! And that proves conclusively that Columbus is up there in heaven with all the rest of 'em!"

It's the *truth*. The truth must be *maintained!* You must fight for the truth! *Columbus was the first man to plant a flag on our hemisphere!* See, I'm talking here like a man of thirty, and I could act like a man of thirty. Maybe I could knock somebody's *puss* down, understand? I still got that in me. You got any more? Go ahead, ask 'em. I'll answer 'em all for you. Go ahead, shoot. I could take it. ■

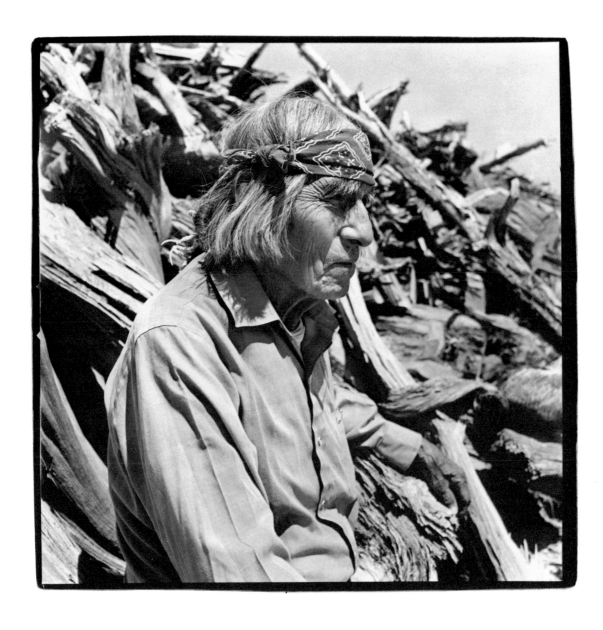

Mike Gashwazra
RELIGIOUS LEADER
OLD ORAIBI, HOPI INDIAN RESERVATION, ARIZONA

The Hopi village of Oraibi, founded around 900 A.D., is the oldest continuously inhabited town in North America, and Mike Gashwazra, eighty-eight years old when we met him, is the oldest man living in the continent's oldest town.

Nearly five thousand people live on the Hopi Indian Reservation, a dozen villages perched atop three sandstone mesas in northeastern Arizona. The oldest of these villages, Oraibi, sits on the westernmost of these cliffs, Third Mesa. Oraibi looks its thousand years—a single dirt road snakes through tightly packed rows of ancient stone houses, many seeming ready to crumble. There are some modern cinder-block houses in the town as well, simple structures, like the one Mike Gashwazra lives in at the very edge of the mesa, looking over the vast swathes of bean, watermelon, and squash fields below.

Mike Gashwazra, Oraibi's religious leader, is also the leader of the village's "traditionalist" faction—fighting the town's mostly younger progressives to keep running water and electricity out of the village. It is one of the last towns in the country resisting these modern conveniences. "The reason why we don't want the electricity and water is because of the farming we do here," Gashwazra explained, switching between broken English and Hopi, with his daughter Angelita translating. "If the electricity should come in, it will take the place of the warm sun, and the sun might not give us any more heat. Why we don't want running water is the same thing: we pray to the rain gods a lot, and that's where we get our water. If we accept running water up here, our prayers will not reach the rain gods. They'll not give us any water, and the farming will go down. We'll be dancing for nothing."

The conflict between the traditionalists and progressives has been raging in Oraibi for at least a century, with traditionalists resisting anything having to do with the ways of the "bahanna," or the white man. In 1906, the conflict became so heated that it caused a split in the town: a group of traditionalists left Oraibi and created the nearby village of Hotevilla, also on Third Mesa. (That community continues to refuse running water and electricity as well.) Some traditionalists remained in what became known as Old Oraibi.

Mike Gashwazra speaks a few words to his daughter, who turns toward me. "He doesn't want to talk anymore," she tells me. "He's saying he's worried that the people will say, 'Why is he telling the white people these things that they don't need to know?'" ■

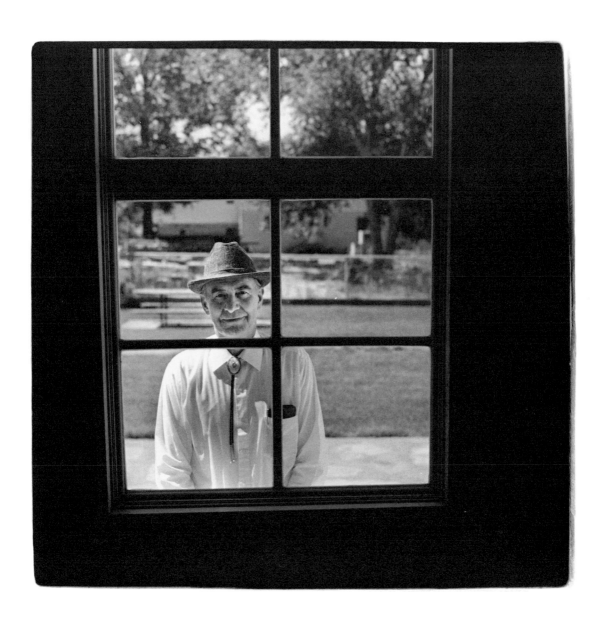

Dan Barlow
FUNDAMENTALIST MORMON AND MAYOR
COLORADO CITY, ARIZONA

For sixty years, a remote tract of land on the Arizona side of the Utah-Arizona border has been home to a community of Fundamentalist Mormons, many of whom practice polygamy (they call it "plural marriage") as a matter of religious conviction. Today several thousand believers live in Colorado City, a dusty town of modest homes and a few stores surrounded by dramatic vermilion cliffs. The residents are clean-cut, well-dressed, and polite. They're also extremely suspicious of outsiders.

The Mormon practice of polygamy dates back to the early 1840s, when Mormon founder Joseph Smith, Jr., reported that he had received revelations from God that plural marriage must be practiced in the present ("latter days"), much as it had been in biblical times. These revelations were published in Doctrines and Covenants *(1843), one of the principal sacred texts of the Mormon Church.*

In 1852, Mormons went public with their belief in plural marriage. The reaction around the country was swift. Violent anti-Mormon rhetoric became a mainstay of political platforms and tabloid newspapers. Increasingly severe anti-polygamy laws were passed. Mormons were fined and imprisoned. In 1880, President Hayes recommended that Mormons be stripped of their citizenship. In 1890, the Supreme Court approved a congressional act allowing for the seizure of all Mormon property. Finally the church relented.

On September 24, 1890, Mormon President Wilford Woodruff issued a statement known as "the manifesto," which forbade plural marriages. The church issued another, stronger antipolygamy statement, "the second manifesto" in 1904. In 1935 the church issued "the final manifesto," which stated that any Mormon who practiced polygamy would be immediately excommunicated from the church, and required all suspected polygamists to sign an oath renouncing the practice of plural marriage. That same year, a group of several hundred renegade Fundamentalist Mormons settled the town of Short Creek, Arizona (which was later renamed Colorado City). Today Colorado City and its sister city of Hilldale, just across the state line in Utah, make up the largest community of Fundamentalist Mormons in the world, with a population of just over five thousand.

With the help of an attorney named Ken Driggs, who is probably the nation's leading outside authority on Fundamentalist Mormons, I visited Colorado City in June of 1992. I spent several hours interviewing the town's mayor, Dan Barlow, about the community, and specifically about an event known as the Short Creek Raid. On July 26, 1953, more than one hundred law enforcement officers raided Short Creek, arresting the entire town and taking away all of the children. At the time, it was the largest police action in Arizona history. In Colorado City, the story is told and retold. The raid is the defining event in the history of the community.

While I was familiar with the story, Dan Barlow's delivery took me by surprise. Up to that point, Mayor Barlow had been exceedingly polite, formal, and guarded, like the others I met that day in Colorado City. But as he recounted the raid, Mayor Barlow began to weep. He wept through much of the telling.

I'm Mayor Dan Barlow of Colorado City. In 1953 I was twenty-one years old. The weekend of the raid started out as a celebration. The 24th of July is Pioneer Day in Mormon Country, was the day that Brigham Young settled in the Salt Lake Valley, so we were celebrating on Friday. Saturday the 25th some folks come from Salt Lake and told us the authorities were planning a raid for that weekend. So we were somewhat prepared, but where can you run? We had no idea what was going to happen, we just heard there was going to be a raid on our people.

So late that evening, towards midnight, some of us younger fellows went out and sat on what we call the Berry Knoll—it's kind of a lookout point about two miles straight south of town. We just sat there and watched. Finally at about twelve o'clock we saw one set of lights coming up the old county road. It pulled up within about thirty feet of me and stopped. It was a sheriff's station wagon, just sitting there blocking the road not letting anybody in or out. That's when I realized they were actually going to do it—I didn't think it was going to happen before then. So we returned into town, and warned the community.

So, some of the leaders in the community called together the people, and we had a meeting in the middle of the night here in the old school building. We were told at that time that the raid was coming, and they didn't know what was going to happen, but they encouraged the people to hold the faith, keep calm, and just depend on the Lord.

Near towards four in the morning, I said to a couple of the other boys, "Let's go back out to the knoll and see what happened." We hiked through the fields, and crawled up carefully through the brush until we was about fifteen feet from that highway patrol car. And I was laying there on my belly listening to them talking, when I felt the ground start to rumble. I wondered what was going on, and I noticed in the moonlight, down the old county road, a great line of cars coming with their lights off—they had figured that they were going to come in and take the community by surprise. I turned to the fellows that was with me and said to them, "I'm going to get back into town and warn the people," and they said,

"All right, we'll stay here." And I took off and run that distance back—I wanted to beat the cars in.

And so I came and told President Johnson—our Prophet at that time—that there were hundreds of cars, hundreds of policemen. The highway patrol was there, and the National Guard. And at that time we rung the bell to call the people together, and the folks returned to the schoolyard. The officers then, recognizing that the element of surprise was totally gone, decided that they would come in with a show. And so, as we stood here in this very square right here watching and wondering what was coming next, we saw police cars start coming over the hill. They were about two miles long—a steady stream of lights and sirens, and they just come in like a Gestapo.

As they drove up, someone struck up the chord and began to sing "God Bless America." Somebody else said, "Run up the flag," and they run Old Glory to the top. And as they come by the schoolyard, the sheriff yelled out on his loudspeaker: "Everybody stay where you are—you're all under arrest!" And the officers got out and circled us completely with their shotguns.

They didn't find what they thought. When they come in here the people were singing "God Bless America.". . . [weeps] It's difficult for me to even talk about it after all these years because of the emotional experience it was to me. . . . Our leader, Mr. Johnson, stepped up and he spoke very sternly. He said, "You are making an injustice against an innocent people. For had you sent word to us, we would have been at any place, we would have responded to any kind of a court order—because that's our nature!" Grandpa Jessup, the patriarch of the community at that time, was eighty-four years old. He was a fearless old man with a long white beard, and he stepped forward and said, "If it's blood you want, take mine. I'm not afraid."

They held us in the little school here as they got the paperwork together. They had warrants for arrest for every man and woman in the community. They declared all the children neglected and dependent. So they took my children—the court ordered them to take my three little children, because I was teaching them to break the law of the land. . . . My baby was ten days old. . . . I didn't know what they were going to do. They informed us that they were going to take the men and put them in jail, take the women and put them in detention homes, and take the children and adopt them out and destroy the records so that they couldn't ever be traced again.

But we held our peace. Our leader said that we will fight this in the courts. He didn't want any kind of violence, and he didn't want any kind of retaliation. Our leader told the men, "The law will take care of us, and the Lord will preserve us." And that's what we did. We fought our way through the court, and we won. After a long severe struggle, they dismissed the cases against the ladies, they dismissed the cases against most of the men, and the courts, finally after two years of grinding, returned the children. Thank God for America, and that it has a way of righting its wrongs!

Short Creek turned into a nightmare for Arizona Governor Howard Pile who had orchestrated the high-profile raid. While newspapers across the country initially praised the efforts, the Arizona public quickly soured on the notion of removing children from their mothers, polygamists or not. The incident is widely regarded as ending Governor Pile's political career. He never won another election. Since the raid, the state of Arizona has kept its distance from Colorado City.

I proposed that this oral history segment be aired on NPR on the fortieth anniversary of the Short Creek Raid. This was soon after the Branch Davidians incident in Waco, and the editorial desk at the network was skittish about the piece. They had questions about long-floating rumors of child abuse, tax fraud, and economic servitude within the community, and thought it lacked balance. Soon thereafter, I received a letter from Ken Driggs, the attorney who had originally introduced me to the people of Colorado City:

"When I first started visiting the community I was told a lot of really malicious things about Short Creek by people who may have been well intended but had little or no basis for their reports. What I have found convinces me that the real secret is how ordinary Short Creek life is. They are similar to Amish, Hutterite, or Mennonite people. These people are deeply religious, they are devoted to their families, and they are intensely patriotic. People in Short Creek have been so maligned that they often shrink from contact with the outside world. Such a situation has a way of perpetuating the rumors. Like many other cultural minorities in our country, the Fundamentalist Mormons of Short Creek have never been allowed to tell their story as they believe it. I would hope NPR would be clear-sighted enough to understand the difference between balance and perpetuating religious prejudice."

The story of the Short Creek Raid never made it to air. ■

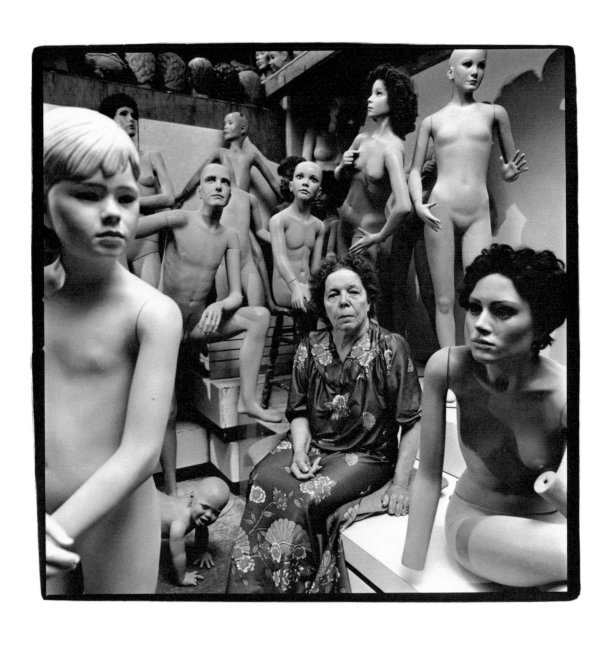

Evangeline "Van" Calvin
Mannequin Restorer
Portland, Oregon

Ever on the lookout for interesting, endangered, and/or strange occupations, Harvey and I ventured to Van Calvin Mannequin Repair to meet Evangeline Calvin, the country's premier mannequin restorer. You can't miss her shop: a big display window jammed with mannequins on U.S. 30, about ten miles northwest of downtown Portland. It's an eerie place: piles of limbs, bags of hair, oddly posed mannequins of all shapes and sizes—each one naked but for an occasional necktie or open robe. The faces are meticulously painted and unusually lifelike: smiling, confused, thoughtful, sexy—the mark of a Van Calvin restoration.

We met Ms. Calvin soon after she had suffered a series of small strokes that caused her to lose much of her memory. Her son, Mikel, and his friend Russ Varner had taken over the bulk of the restoration work, although Van did continue to paint an occasional mannequin face. Ms. Calvin was spunky, charming, and clearly frustrated at her inability to remember details of her life and career.

VAN CALVIN: My name is Evangeline Maude Calvin. I am ninety. No, I'm not ninety yet. I'm eighty. I got started in this business kind of accidentally on purpose. . . . Well, fact of the matter is, I guess I don't remember what happened. . . .

MIKEL CALVIN: I'm not important here, but you can get the chronology from me, and maybe she can remember and then tell it. Mother always did anything you could do with art. She would paint huge murals—take a five-inch-wide brush and paint the side of a building just like most people would brush their teeth, she's always been very talented for that. She used to work in a photography studio retouching photos, and that's what she did during the war. When I was twelve and she was early-middle-aged, we got to Southern California. We were hungry. We didn't have anything to do. She went looking for a job in a photography studio, and met this fella in this big warehouse named Krasner, who had a huge pile of mannequins. They got to talking and he said, "Do you think you could put a face on 'em and make 'em look like I could sell 'em? 'Cause right now they're just a bunch of disjointed parts."

VAN: There were a lot of them! Maybe twenty-five or thirty in this one room no bigger than this, just stacked all up. . . .

MIKEL: Maybe two or three hundred!

VAN: [Laughs] Yeah, a whole bunch! So we started doin' 'em. . . . [Fades off]

MIKEL: She said to me: "Climb in there and grab me that bottom, and we'll take this top, and we'll take these arms over here, and that looks like a pair of hands that would fit on there." And we managed to piece together five of them, and took them home, and repaired 'em. We used plaster of Paris and glue and newspaper and sticks—whatever would work—and then she'd put a pretty face on it. And from what had been a pile of junk, like a genie, voilà, there was suddenly a beautiful mannequin. We got twenty-five dollars for that load, and that was well toward paying the rent, so we continued doing it.

Now we get one hundred and forty dollars minimum to repair a mannequin. If it's damaged beyond that, we charge more, like we charge eight-fifty to reaffix a finger that's been broken off, or twelve-fifty to make a new one. But what really distinguishes us is our beautiful hand-painted faces. So many of the factories have ten artists in an assembly line that spray on the faces with an airbrush, and they have that plastic sex-doll look. But you can always recognize mother's faces.

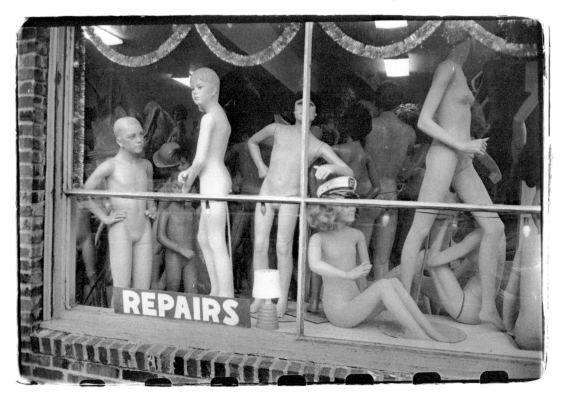

Big eyes—like deer—great big pupils and irises, and a kind of a dreamy, sweet expression. They all look back at you with these big eyes. . . .

VAN: [Laughs] It's a funny job, in a way, because . . . hmm. . . . You poor kid, I'm ashamed of myself. I'm being so stupid. . . .

MIKEL: He meets a lot of stupid people. . . .

VAN: There was a man named Krasner. He had this room full of mannequins. There was a pile of arms over here, and a bunch of bottoms over there, and legs there. And each one was just a screwed-up mess. So I said, "Well, we'll just start here." And that's what we did. . . . But, um . . . the thing about it is, any mannequin we ever did came out about the best we could do it. That's what makes it, isn't it? If you're trying your best all the time? Whatever it takes to get a job done, I can do it. I know I can do it. Can't I?

MIKEL: That's the wisdom she instilled in me.

Mikel Calvin died of AIDS a couple of months after this interview. Van Calvin left the shop, and now lives with her daughter, Michaele. ▮

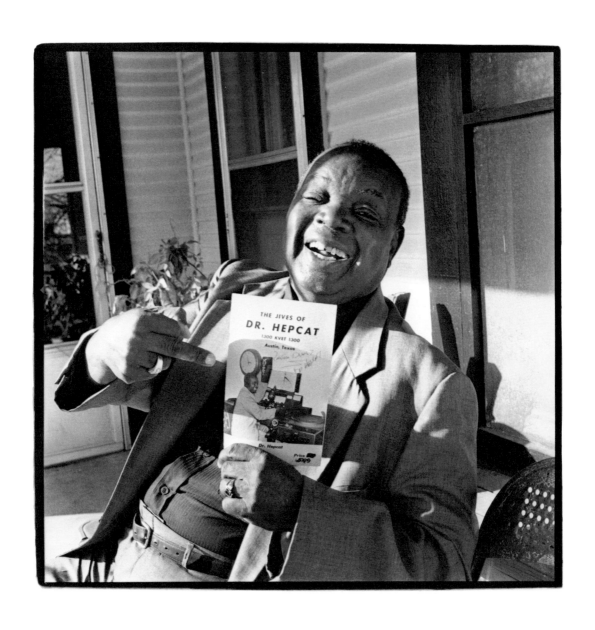

The Rev. Lavada Durst, a.k.a. Dr. Hepcat
Disc Jockey (Retired)
Austin, Texas

In the 1930s, the Reverend Lavada Durst of Austin, Texas, was better known as Dr. Hepcat, the first African-American disc jockey in the state and the nation's leading expert on "jive talk," the dialect fashionable among young African-Americans at the time. In 1953 he published the definitive work on the subject, The Jives of Dr. Hepcat, *a slim but comprehensive volume which carefully lays out the proper use of all "hepster" phrases, and even includes a handy jive talk dictionary at the back. I interviewed Lavada Durst in November 1992, at his home in Mason Town, one of the oldest black communities in Austin.*

I am Reverend A. L. Durst, associate minister at the Olivet Baptist Church. I used to be Dr. Hepcat, one of the coolest cats on the stem, strictly on the beam. I was ready, willing, and able, ace high and qualified. You ask me how old I am? Well, I'm past sixteen, big, black, and mean. [Laughs] Actually, I was born in 1913.

I started my career in 1929, announcing baseball games for the Negro Leagues in Austin, Texas. I was in the box doing play-by-play. The people used to come to the ballpark in droves to hear me do that baseball lingo. This is what you'd hear:

Up to the bat comes Cool Papa Chaney, battin' from the South Side—he's a cool cat from way back. In come the ball like a little bitty pea. It's gobbled up by the shortstop, over to first base. He's out! That shortstop has a rifle on him! He's a groundkeeping shortstop—boy, he's on the beam!

Nobody's out, nobody on base. The score is tied nothing to nothing. The pitcher, Sweet Slumber Walker, winds up. Here comes the ball—fast like a lightning bolt. Phshhh—striiiiike called!

That's about it. I'm rusty, see, because my field is a little different now. I can talk about the Lord now just like I did baseball then.

Well, in 1935, some of the powers that be at the radio station KVET heard me, and gave me the chance to be one of the first black DJs not only in Texas but also in a lot of other places, with my own show. It was called *Rosewood Ramble*, named after a street in East Austin called Rosewood Avenue where there were lots of clubs for blacks.

What you hear? I came on with Duke Ellington's "Things Aint What They Used to Be." Then:

Hey there, chappie, 'lo chicks. You've latched on to *Rosewood Ramble,* with your music recorded. It's a real gone deal that I'm gonna wield, so stand by while I pad your skulls. This record's by a big cool kitty from Bop City, he's on the beam with no parts lame. He's a cat that'll rack 'em back, Nat King Cole with a mad stack. Pick up on the Nat—here he is.

When I first got on the air I had to be a little bit different—so I talked in jive talk. It was just the way we'd communicate with each other to keep other people from knowing what we were talking about—we had a language of our own. And I was a master of that jive talk, so I called myself Dr. Hepcat.

Now this is Hepcat's prayer. We normally say it at night—at sleepytime:

I stash me down to cop a nod. I put my mellow frame upon the sod. If I should cop a drill before the early toot, I lay a spill on the head knock to make everything allroot. So with that fly cat, I chill my chat and fall back to my righteous pad and cop a nod like mad.

It's hard for me, because my chops is not putting out the gas like I want them to—that means I can't talk like I want to because my mouth can't hit those words like it used to do. Lordy! Sometimes I bump into the old-timers, then we go into a gabfest of those days—reminiscing.

Rosewood Ramble was supposed to be only for the blacks, but I found out I had a lot of white listeners too—they was listening! So I would say, "It's music for everybody on the face of this revolving globe." The program director made me stop saying that, though, because he wanted to keep it black—you understand. But it got out! It got out, oh yes.

'Course, you know it was kind of tough—to be black and be on the white man's radio. Sometimes they'd have to walk me out the back alley to keep somebody from throwing a rock at me, but I made it. In spite of the trials and knocks I received, I had to stay there to keep the door open for the others to come along. I held the door open. And everywhere you go today you hear blacks—women and men—on the air! You cannot stop progress! ■

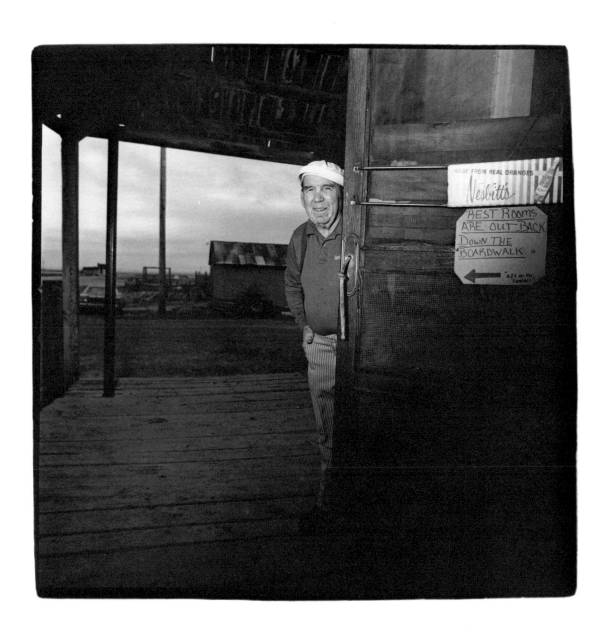

Bill Seward
OWNER, JERSEY LILLY BAR AND CAFE
INGOMAR, MONTANA

We pulled into the ghost town of Ingomar, a little after midnight one evening in November 1993. Dust balls blew up and down Main Street. Abandoned buildings creaked in the wind. It was pitch-dark, but for a light in the Jersey Lilly Cafe: Ingomar's sole business, located in the town's only intact building. In the early 1900s it was the First State Bank. Back then, Ingomar was a boomtown, home to the world's second-largest sheep-shearing plant, and hundreds of residents. A fire in the early 1920s burned down every building in town except the bank, and set in motion Ingomar's rapid decline. Today, only eighteen people remain, including Bill Seward, proprietor of the Jersey Lilly.

Outside: two old gas pumps, a hitching post, his and her outhouses. Inside: creaky floors, a long bar, moose heads on the walls and spittoons on the floor. Bill Seward, one-time professional boxer, stocky but still strong, is seventy-four when we meet him. He wears a white sailor cap, dirty yellow suspenders, and checkered pants. ("Some people think it's my only pants, but I got six of the same pair and I wear a different one every day.") High on his nose rest Seward's trademark eyeglasses. A string runs up from the bridge and loops around his head. ("So I don't have to keep pushin' 'em up all the time. This way your ears don't hurt and you don't get saddle sores on your nose.") While Seward's clientele, mostly hunters and ranchers passing through Ingomar, can be sparse, the hours he keeps are not: officially open from 6:00 A.M. until 2:00 A.M. If you happen to show up later, he'll be glad to fix you a bowl of his famous Jersey Lilly beans or fill your gas tank.

When we arrive at the Jersey Lilly, Bill is taking a nap in the cellar under the trapdoor behind the bar; that's where he lives. We rouse him and spend several hours talking and eating. The beans are unforgettable.

Excuse me, I'm just gonna go right over here and brush my teeth. I had to get a little sleep. You had quite a trip, a lot of driving. You come from Butte? That's quite a town. One time they had nine professional fighters living and working out of Butte, and they'd have maybe two fight cards a day. Big cards. John L. Sullivan was there, and a lot of them younger guys—middleweights. A terrific fight town.

Me? I was born and raised right here in Ingomar. My dad, he come up here as a young fellow from Texas, and he met my mother here—she come with her folks from Michigan as homesteaders. 1919, I guess it was, when I was supposed to be born—didn't have any birth certificate. It was a big sheep-shearing center then, and they had this big shearing plant up here with conveyor belts and all that. Then they had the fire in '21. Burnt down twenty-three business places including five hotels and two rooming houses and a mission. Just everything: grocery stores, barbershops, pool halls, livery stables, feed stores. Only thing that didn't burn was the building we're in right now, the bank, even though it went broke that same year and sat empty for years.

Daddy got appointed deputy sheriff here in 1914, but mostly my family was horse people. Filly chasers. We'd take wild horses, unbroken horses, and we'd break 'em and sell 'em. I hung my saddle up in 1936, and went to Chicago to learn to be a professional boxer. I fought as a lightweight, and I was pretty good. Had eight consecutive one-round knockouts. All together thirty-eight knockouts in forty-five fights, and only lost one. My last fight was in October of '41, and then I was subject to the draft, so I dropped everything and went into the service. Never did fight again. After you get away from boxing for five years you don't go back. A year at most, maybe. After five years, you're dead.

My dad opened this place up back in '48. One night at 'bout nine o'clock my dad sent my sister up the street to the bar—it was the only business in town at the time—to get him some cigarettes, and they was closed. That made the old gentleman a little bit perturbed—he figured it was nicer to spit in church than to close a bar at nine at night, you know, so he said, "By God, I'll open up my own joint!" So I come back here to help him open it up, and I just stayed.

He called this place the Jersey Lilly after Judge Bean's place. My dad came from Texas, and he was familiar with the old judge Roy Bean, and he kind of run this town like old Bean run his. Daddy had a boxcar for a jail, and when he had guys he didn't like, he'd just put them in jail and ship that car out to Mile City or Roundup and get rid of 'em. None of 'em come back to haunt him. It was kind of a fun thing for Daddy. He was a good deputy sheriff. Anyway, when this place got too much for him, I took it over.

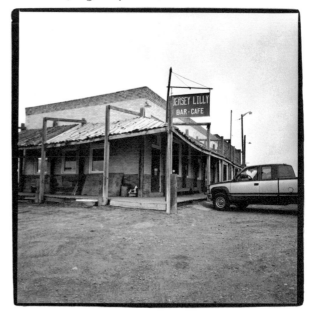

Now this is your famous sheepherder's hors d'oeuvres. Take one onion, one cracker, and one piece of orange and stick it all in your mouth one bite, just like an old hound dog eating hot cakes. Don't taste a thing like you thought it would, do it? What a surprise! You never did eat nothin' like that, did ya? Try some more. . . . And here's a bowl of our beans, Jersey Lilly style. Our beans are really special. Internationally famous they are. Beans are one of finest foods there is. Most places don't do anything for them—just boil 'em up with salt water and serve 'em out. See, I cook 'em today for tomorrow. If you cook 'em the day before and let 'em set, the flavor gets all the way through the beans. Otherwise the flavor's just in the juice. Beans are very fragile, see. It's amazing how many people have never eaten beans that they liked. They remember these.

To me, this place is the hub of the universe. That might sound kind of funny, but that's how I feel. It agrees with me. After five years in Chicago and five years in the service, I know where I want to be. I can look out the window and see for seventy miles. There's no rocks, no clouds, no clutter, no trees—there's nothing but space. No confinement, nothing hemming you in. And, I'll tell you, if I didn't like it here, I'd just leave. Wouldn't even bother shuttin' the door. I'd just walk right off. That's the way I am about it. ■

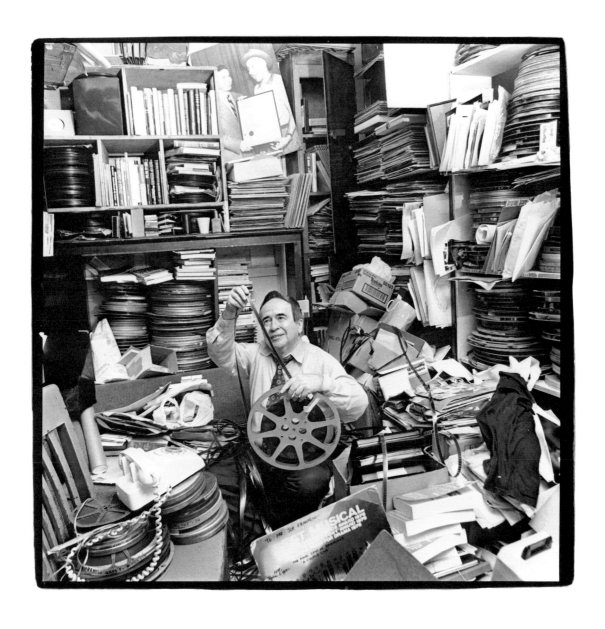

Joe Franklin
TALK SHOW HOST
NEW YORK CITY

Over the years Harvey and I have met some pretty impressive characters. Unbelievable characters. But if I had to pick the greatest of them all, it would have to be talk show host Joe Franklin. Just give a call to his office (the number's listed), and you'll see what I mean: "Hello? Who's this?" he'll ask. "[Fill in your name], my friend!" he'll exclaim, as if he's known you all his life. "Listen to me closely now—whatever you want it's automatic. Listen, [Fill in your name]—I'm very busy. Very busy. Call me back at three o'clock exactly. You swear? Don't forget now—very important. Critical! God bless you." SLAM. "I get about 1,000 calls a day from people who want to be on my show," Joe explains. "Of course, most of them can't be on, but I hate to hurt their feelings so I never say 'good-bye.' I just hang up. So that way they feel the conversation hangs in limbo until we chat again."

A JOE FRANKLIN TELEPHONE SAMPLER
(Recorded 8/91)

Richard! Richard! I got a lot of good news for you, Richard. Listen carefully: you call me reverse charges at seven o'clock, and I'll be here. You promise me, Richard? Richard, I got so many surprises for you. Let's talk tonight at seven o'clock. Very important, Richard! [Slam]

Dan! How are you, my boy? Dan, I need you maniacally! Pathologically! Desperately! I'm standing by, Dan. Keep me close, Danny. Keep me notified! [Slam]

Sophie! What is your informed appraisal? What is your educated assessment? What is your considered opinion? Do you see things concretizing? Are they coming together? Are they coagulating? Listen, I got more to tell you, and I'm talking on the other phone, so we're gonna talk in a little while. Promise? God bless you, Sophie, I won't forget you for this. [Slam]

Greg? Listen, Greg, I think the concept is *sensational!* I got a couple of private investors and I got a couple of what you might call "patron of the art" subsidizing-type philanthropists. Even without star quality, without the big names, I think the concept of the project is *sensational.* We'll swing something.

Listen, Greg, listen, boss, I swear to you I'll have good news for you at four o'clock. Guaranteed. My word of honor—exactly four P.M. Call me at four sharp. And if I have something sooner, I'll call you more abruptly. [Slam]

Penny! Now listen, I'm getting my schedule tomorrow. Give me till Friday morning ten o'clock. Promise? Don't run away. I swear, don't run away! Wait there! [Slam]

Yeah, listen, I got a man here who's doing a big, big profile of me for public radio. Should I bring him over and whatever you say about your company will be heard by millions of people? Okay, kid? We'll see you in about five minutes or less, all right, boss? [Slam]

We never went.

A steady stream of oddballs amble in and out all day for "meetings." In the midst of all this, I somehow managed to eek out an interview. I produced a tribute to the Great One in August 1990, as he was gearing up to celebrate the fortieth anniversary of the Joe Franklin Show.

Okay, my boy? Oh, this is gonna be a big show. Gigantic! You'll get plenty of good stuff! Can't miss! Can't miss! My voice is shot—I had about a thousand phone calls this morning. [Clears his throat] Okay, my name is Joe Franklin. I work for my brother, my brother's out of a job right now, but we'll hit a home run at the top of the ninth. Okay? Ready?

Well, I've been doing radio and TV now for about forty-one years. I began in radio working for a man named Martin Block on a program called *The Make-Believe Ballroom* in about 1950 on that station called WNEW—they were a very important station then—they were number one! I was his record picker, and he took a liking to me. He got me my own radio show every night following his. I called my show *Vaudeville Isn't Dead* and I went out to all the different stores and I bought old records by Al Jolson, and Eddie Cantor and Bing Crosby. I paid a penny apiece. Then I'd go on the radio and say, "Ladies and gentlemen, here's a collector's item by Al Jolson, which is worth five hundred dollars." I'd make up these crazy astronomical, maniacal figures. Then I'd go back to the store the next day to buy four more records. I put four pennies down at the counter and the dealer would say, "Hey kid! Come here, kid! I heard somebody on the radio last night saying these records were worth five hundred dollars apiece." So I unwittingly, single-handedly created what you would call "the rare record market." I think I also created the word "collectible." I *think* I was the first. I *know* that I was the first one to apply the word "nostalgia" to show business. And I was the first one to popularize the phrase "memory lane." So I'm now part of the psyche, I'm a legend in my own room. I guess you could say I'm semi-immortal. I have semi-superstar status.

I'm probably by now the longest-running show on television. I think there was a show called *Meet the Press.* They still on? I don't know. Well, then I guess I'm second, but I'm certainly the longest-running talk show. I think I created the talk show as we know it because when I began there were no talk shows. Channel 7 at that time asked me if I wanted to occupy an hour a day in television, and I said, "I'd be happy to." So they said, "If we give you an hour a day, what kind of show would you do, Joe?" I said, "Well, how about if I do a show of people talking—nose to nose, eyeball to eyeball, face to face, toe to toe." They said, "Joe, who's gonna watch people talking? The word is tele-*vision!* You got to give them *vision!* Got to give them seltzer bottles, pratfalls, got to give them baggy pants, got to give them *movement!*" Rock and roll was just getting big then, so I said, "Well, if I can't do that, how about if I do a show with kids dancing to records?" They said, "Joe, now we know you're nuts! Who's gonna watch kids dancing to records?" (So comes along Dick Clark, a billionaire today!) Anyhow, I defied them, and I did the first TV talk show. And look what it is today—everybody in the country wants to do a TV talk show today.

I've had 'em all! Two hundred and fifty thousand guests in forty years! I read in magazines about people who never did talk shows: Cary Grant never did one, James Cagney never did one, John Wayne, John Lennon, Elvis Presley. I've got the photographs and old kinescopes to show that these people were on *my* show. I gave the first exposure to Barbra Streisand, Flip Wilson, Bill Cosby, Eddie Murphy, Liza Minnelli, Robert Redford, Dustin Hoffman, Bruce Springsteen, Joan Rivers. And I try to give the little guy a shot, too, whenever I can. But it's getting harder and harder—you're fighting a ratings war nowadays! I've had dancing dentists. Singing lawyers. I have had people who play the piano standing on their heads. I've had cab drivers who do handwriting analysis—you name it, I've had it. And if I haven't had it, I'll create it.

People call all day to get on the show. I'll say, "What's your specialty?" They'll say to me, "finance," or "health," or "nutrition," or "romance." I'll say to them,

"What's your qualifications? What's your credentials?" Most of them have hardly any! In other words, they've got a need to be rejected. I try to be nice to them. I try to steer them to a smaller show, or I say, "Let me think about it," or "I'm in repeats right now," or "I'm sick with the dentist." I really try not to hurt their feelings. And if the person is driven and he makes a little bit of sense, I'll try to help him out. If a guy calls maybe nine hundred times and wears me down, he'll generally get on my show.

The telephone never stops. Once or twice a year the phone actually explodes, like an artery, like a heart attack. There might be nine hundred people trying to get through that line at one time and it actually gets a stroke and the dial blows out—believe it or not! You hear that out there? It never stops. [Aside to his assistant] I'll be there in a second. Tell him half a minute. [Back to interview] I'm a good juggler of people, see.

I think I'm the last host who's "organic" or "from the bones." Never had an agent, never had a manager. If I was part of the machine, I'm sure I'd be worth eighty million dollars today. Not that I have any complaints—I'm eating well, I'm not wasting away, right? I'm not withering. I try to look in the guests' eyes, not their nose or their belly button. I would venture to say I'm the only talk show host in the world that isn't rehearsed and does not have a preproduction meeting. On most talk shows when somebody asks, "How do you feel?" it says on a card, "FINE." I figure if you're gonna have dinner in a restaurant, you don't rehearse your dialogue before the meal, right? So I go along with that. I just let it flow, and somehow it works. I think there have been four hundred talk show hosts in New York City alone who came and went since I began—*four hundred!* So I must be doing something right. And I'm at the peak of it now. They tell me with cable I have between four and twelve million people watching me *every night*. Why tamper with success, right?

Despite his assurances to the contrary, in 1993 The Joe Franklin Show *went off the air. When I spoke with Joe in July 1994, he assured me that he'd soon be making his return to the small screen. "As of now I've got fifteen actually* pleading *offers on the table to return to five-day-a-week TV!" he said. "These are from fifteen of the top TV executives! Top! They're all after me. Big people, big people. Virtually begging me!" Come back soon, Joe. It's critical.* ■

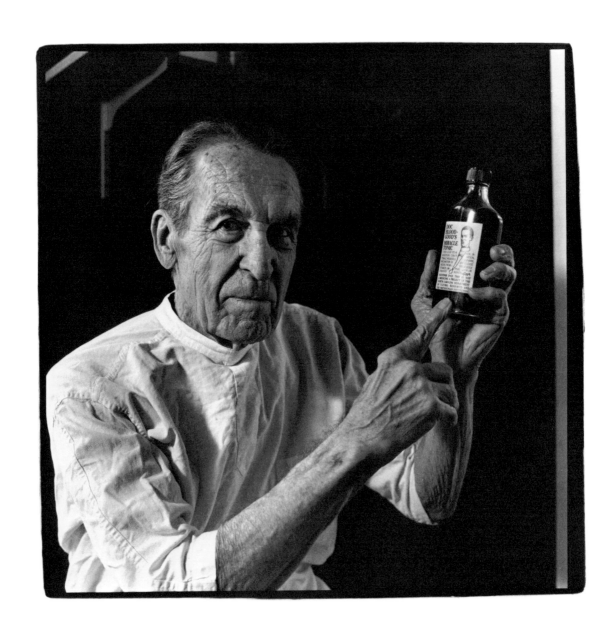

Fred Bloodgood
Side-Show Pitchman (Retired)
Madison, Wisconsin

To this day, Fred Bloodgood speaks with a showman's oratorical flourishes. "It would be the high point of my career to have the honor of meeting you," he proclaimed, when I called him at his home in Madison, Wisconsin, in the summer of 1992 to see if he might want to do an interview. "Each moment of waiting will be like a thousand hours. I can honestly tell you that from now on I will look back on my life as one divided between two eras: before you called and after you called."

Fred Bloodgood spent most of his career working as a typewriter salesman for the Remington Company, but has always looked back upon the work he did in the twenties and thirties as his true calling. For about a decade, Bloodgood traveled with a series of carnivals, working as a side-show pitchman for a variety of acts, most notably "Neola, that strangest of all strange creatures." During the off-season, Bloodgood ran a medicine show that traveled through the South. Bloodgood remembers every detail of those days, and in the course of conversation will frequently break into one or another of his pitches—each of which he remembers word for word. "It's strange," he told me, "I can't remember my own telephone number, but I can remember every one of those!"

I'm Fred Bloodgood, and I'm eighty-two years old. The way I got into show business? Well, my dad took me to the circus, and the circus was just great, but to me the sideshow—the sideshow was absolutely inspiring! And at that time I solemnly vowed that if I ever got out of school I would surely become a sideshow talker. I just thought that to be able to stand on that platform in front of a long, long line of pictorial paintings, meanwhile extolling the benefits to be derived by actually witnessing that congress of freaks and curiosities and monstrosities—surely that'd be the greatest occupation a man could ever have!

Well, the day I finished high school—that would have been in 1927—the very next day I hitchhiked to the nearest circus, and in no time I was over on the sideshow. There occurred the most exciting, adventuresome years that a youth could ever have. . . .

"Now ladies and gentlemen, if you'll all come down in close, where you can see and hear. You're now standing in front of the feature attraction of the midway. I'm sure you've heard your friends and neighbors talk about Neola, that strangest of all strange creatures. Brought here during the great evolution trial that took place between the late William Jennings Bryan and Clarence

Darrow, the great criminal lawyer. She was examined at that time and found to have less intelligence than that of the chimpanzee.

Now let me paint for you a word picture of her. She stands about three feet tall. Long, long arms that hang way down below the knees. Eyes that pop out and glare. But I think, and I think you'll agree with me when you go inside, that the most peculiar thing of all about her is the shape of the head: the head tapers at the top just like that of a coconut! Now she doesn't speak any language. Neither walks nor talks, just creeps and crawls, and she spends her lifetime in that steel-bound arena. Down in there now, where you wouldn't expect a dog to live for an hour.

Now all afternoon they've been asking, "When and what time are you going to feed her?" Well, ladies and gentlemen, that time has arrived. When I throw that live chicken you see me now holding down deep into that steel-bound cage, you're going to see a most amazing change come over the old woman. The eyes will dilate, the pupils glow just like two red-hot coals of fire. You'll hear her emit just one long soul-searing scream, and then she'll leap clear across that steel-bound arena, catch that bird between those massive jaws, bite off the head with those long and tusky teeth. And then, ladies and gentlemen, as repulsive as it may sound, you'll see her suck, drain, and draw every drop of blood from that bleeding, throbbing, quivering, pulsating body—with the very same relish that you or I would suck the juice of an orange.

Now, friends, it's way past feeding time. I'm going to sell tickets for three minutes and three minutes only, and then I'm gonna feed her whether one of you go, all of you or none of you go. The price, the price so small you can't afford to miss it. Don't fight the ticket box. Thank you. And there goes another one there. Thank you, sir. . . ."

I guess I should hasten to explain that she was not quite as I mentioned it. Show people have a little tendency to exaggerate, and I admit I did. It wasn't quite all real, no. She wasn't a cliff dweller. Actually, it was a guy named Shorty, and I dressed him in a kimono affair with a long black wig that hid his face, and he became "Neola, that strangest of all strange creatures."

Over the years I had a whole lot of different geeks playing Neola, but Shorty was the best one ever. The others were temperamental, and they were drunks. I found Shorty working at the Vanderberg Brothers Greater Combined Circus. The person that hired Shorty before me was Frank Hall, the manager. He told me that Shorty had a very short memory. He says, "If I send him for a bridle for the pony, and I tell him, 'The bridle is in the blue box,' Shorty will say all the way there, 'Bridle in the blue box, bridle in the blue box,' over and over. And sometimes he forgets by the time he gets to the box even." Well, I had a geek at the time, but he was no good—he didn't care about the work. So I said, "Frank, I've got a deal for you. How would it be if we changed my employee for yours?" He said, "You really want Shorty?" I said, "Yeah." He said, "Well, whoever the other guy is, I'm a winner!" So I got Shorty, and Shorty liked it, and I liked it too! He just seemed to enjoy the work.

He worked in the center of a huge pit constructed of two-by-fours, crawling on his hands and knees. I'd toss the chicken in, and he'd scream and bite off the head. Never saw him get sick in my life. Once in a while he'd scream at somebody, and leap towards them—he was very good at this—he always knew who would scream loudest. Could you imagine these teenage girls screaming? They were walking, talking advertisers. But the crowning feature is once in a great while one of these girls would actually faint. Then my buddy which took tickets and I would run in there and grab her off the ground, and manage to carry her all around the carnival—"Is there a doctor in the crowd? Is there a doctor in the crowd?"—until we had exposed her to hundreds of people. I would defy anybody to pass that up. If you couldn't spend a dime or a quarter to see something like that, you didn't have any imagination at all! I'm not being egotistical when I say that show would top the midway almost every single night of the year, because if you hadn't seen Neola, you hadn't seen the carnival!

Yes, they were wonderful days. I hated to go to bed at night. What I wouldn't give to live it over again. Wouldn't that be great to have it all over again? It's a far cry from selling typewriters and adding machines, I'll tell you. ■

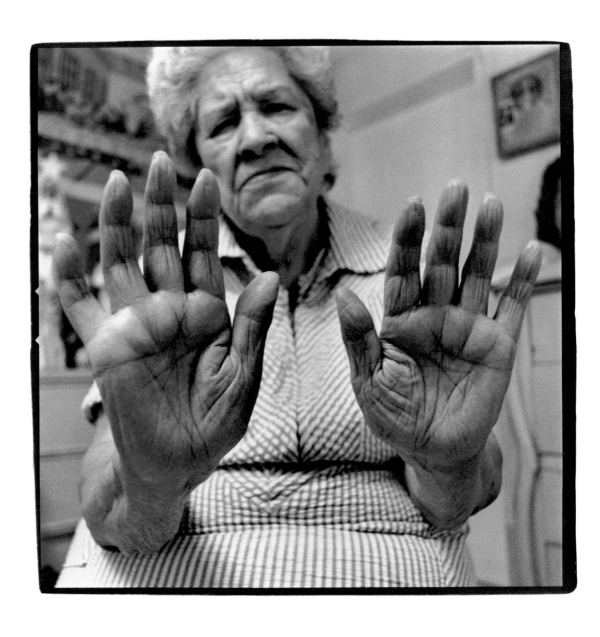

Augustina Martínez
Curandera (Healer)
Alcalde, New Mexico

Augustina Martínez points to her wrinkles as proof. There's the cross on her fore-head, and in her right palm, what at times looks to be an M. It stands, she says, for milagrosa—miracle maker. "It means I can cure anyone," she explains. "Whoever is sick, I touch them with my hands and make them well." Augustina Martínez has been healing people for more than seventy years in the village of Alcalde, one of dozens of small Mexican American enclaves between Taos and Santa Fe. She was eighty-six years old when we met her in November 1993.

I was born with the *virtud*, the knowledge. It's funny, if I see people I could tell if they're sick. I can read it in their faces. Like you're here now and I can look at you and tell you're not sick. But if you were sick I could tell right out. I don't know why or how—it just comes to me.

I was twelve when I deliver my first baby. I never seen nothing like that and I didn't know a thing about it. It came to me that that's the way they birth the babies, so I did it. The doctor was in Santa Fe, and the father went there for him. When the doctor came, he said, "Who took care of you?" And Lola was her name, said, "Tina did." And he look at me very funny. I said, "Did I do something wrong?" And he said, "No, you did a marvelous job." He examined the lady and the baby and it was perfect.

I deliver lots and lots of babies—every day and every night. One time the mother was scared to death because the little hand came out first. She called the doctor, and they wanted to give her a cesarean. I said, "She don't need it. You don't have to call the doctor, I can do it." But she was scared. I put my hand in there and just push a little way, and the baby came out in my hands. And I did-n't know that the doctor was right behind my back, and he said, "How did you deliver that baby?" I said, "I deliver like I deliver every baby." And he said, "But tell me how." And I said, "Someday I will tell you." But I haven't.

There was a girl, she had been a teacher, and she could hardly walk, talk. Her parents had her in the hospital a long time—nothing helped her. They went to every specialist, they even went to Chicago, and nothing doing. Then the moth-er heard about me, and she brought her here. I said, "I'm not a regular doctor, I'm just a médica." And she said, "But I know you could help my girl." The girl came here and in three days she was back teaching. Isn't that a miracle? See, God put things in this world that a lot of people do not appreciate, but I do.

See the cross? See the hands? I have miracle hands. See this eye? Watch my eye. [Laughs] I'm showing you that I have two visions. My eyes are sometimes blue and sometimes brown. They change. When they're brown there's danger. When they're blue, it's a different story. I can see the good and the bad. I can tell when people are lying, when they're telling the truth. That's a miracle.

I don't want people to think I'm a witch—a *bruja*. That's different from what I do. See, I work on the side of God. I'm a Catholic. I don't believe in witches. I hate them, because they make people crippled and blind. You see, I ask God to help me to cure what the evil spirit does. That's what I do. And everybody'd ask the same question—"What are we going to do when you go?" And I say, "God will put somebody in my place. He sent me here, he'll get somebody else." Because it's a miracle that God put me here. Don't you think so? ■

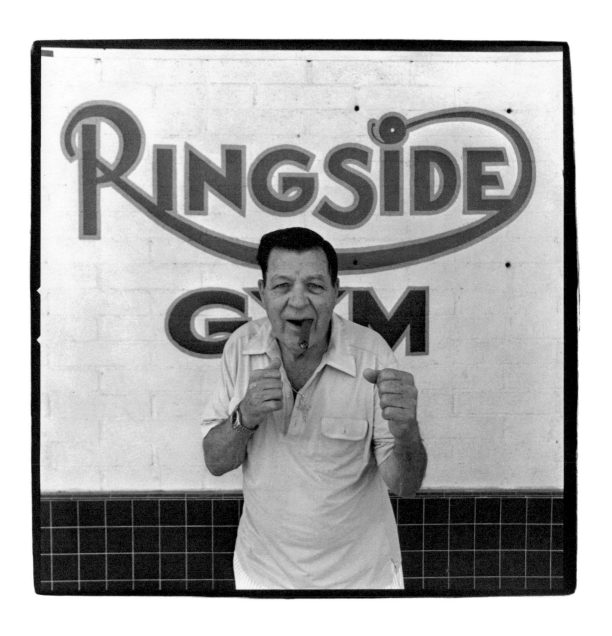

Johnny Tocco
Boxing Trainer and Gym Owner
Las Vegas, Nevada

Johnny Tocco calls a whitewashed box of a building about three miles north of the Vegas casino strip home. At eighty-two, trainer, manager, and gym owner Tocco is the elder statesman of boxing. For more than forty years, he's owned and operated Johnny Tocco's Ringside Gym: Home of the Champions.

It's a stark space. Enter through an iron gate into a front room with a couple of speedbags and a scale. Hang a sharp left, and you've hit the heart of Tocco's operation: a room the fighters call "The Sweat Box." Windowless and stuffy, the Sweat Box is dominated by an old ring, its ropes covered with faded red-white-and-blue bunting, its canvas well-splattered with blood. The old wood-paneled walls are covered with posters and photographs of fighters who've trained here: everyone who's anyone in boxing over the past four decades. They are a constant presence, watching over the fighters, reminders of the Sweet Science at its best. So is Johnny Tocco.

Well, I started in the game when I was nine years old. I had a paper route in St. Louis that went past this old gym, and I'd always stop and look in the door, and I was always chased away by the operator of the gym. One day there was a fighter in there that was getting ready for a fight and he says to the operator, "Hey, quit running that kid out! Come on in here!" And the owner says, "Nah, I don't want the kid in here." So the fighter comes out and grabs my hand and says, "You're gonna be my water boy." I had my papers, and he threw 'em all in the garbage can and says, "Don't worry about it, I'll give you the money for the papers." So I'm in his corner, and every round he says, "Give me the water bottle," and I'd hand him the water bottle, and I thought that was great! So that's how I got my start. Then from a water boy I went to a trainer and then to a manager. Then I opened up my own gym—the Ringside Gym, back in St. Louis in '48—and moved it out to Las Vegas a couple of years after that.

I love the game. I been in it practically all my life, and I'm still goin'. After all, the closest man to me for number of years in the boxing business is Eddie Fugch, and he's eighty-one. I'm gonna turn eighty-three come July. By the way, the name is Tocco—T-O-C-C-O, but everyone calls me Taco. It's always "Hey, Taco!" this and "Hey, Taco!" that, but there's no 'a' in my name, see. I asked Howard Cosell one time, "How come you call me Taco?" He says, "If I called you Tocco nobody'd know who I'm talkin' about." Not too long ago they opened up a new taco joint up the street here, and I got all kinds of people saying, "Hey, that's a beautiful place you opened up! We went in and ate last night!" I said, "Hey, those ain't my restaurants. I have nothing to do with them." I wish I did.

This is the oldest operatin' gym in the world. I been on this corner forty years, and never closed the joint down once. Always open, six days a week, and sometimes seven. Here we have some old fight pictures of the fighters that've worked here from one time or another. You can see we got Larry Holmes, we got Tyson. Holyfield. Ken Norton. Marvin Haggler—this was his home away from home. Over here you can see Sugar Ray Leonard, Leon Spinks, Burbick. Every top champion in the world has been here. They all come here to work.

There's Sonny Liston. I was training him when he died, you know. What happened to him—he was supposed to come to my house for Christmas and he never showed up. We kept waitin' and waitin' and waitin'—and seven days later they found him dead. They went in his house and they found him sittin' on the edge of his bed, with his head back and blood all comin' out of his nose and his mouth. People say that the mob killed him, but I know the mob didn't do it. Still, I get calls from all over the world: "Do you still believe Liston died of a convulsion?" And I say, "Yes, that's my story. I don't think the mob had anything to do with it." Sonny Liston. He finished up his career with me.

This is a gym that gives fighters "incentive." It's not a pretty gym, it's a dirty gym, but this is what it's all about for getting where you want to go in the boxing game. It *looks* like an old-time gym. It's like back in the old days when the gyms was up on the second floor or in a garage or an old firehouse or something like that. They can train here without any disturbances. For instance, I don't allow women in here. If a girl is sittin' there, the fighter's always watchin' to see who's talkin' to her, what she's doin', and it disrupts his training. No women. No visitors bothering you. Nobody poking at you. So it's the complete atmosphere here, I mean you know you're in a boxing gym, and you feel at home.

I've had three of them heart operations. I got a nitro patch and a pacemaker that I've had for three years. But every time something happens I come out of it, and I'll keep comin' out of it. Just last week I had two offers from people that figure I'm gonna quit and wanna take the place over. I always tell them, "What'll happen to me? If I quit, in a coupla weeks they'll be throwin' sand in my face." So, I gotta keep goin'. When the dear Lord comes and puts a hand on my shoulder and says, "Let's take a walk, Johnny," *that'll* be it. But until then I can't see me alive and not workin' with the fight game. I'd be lost. ∎

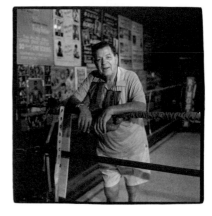

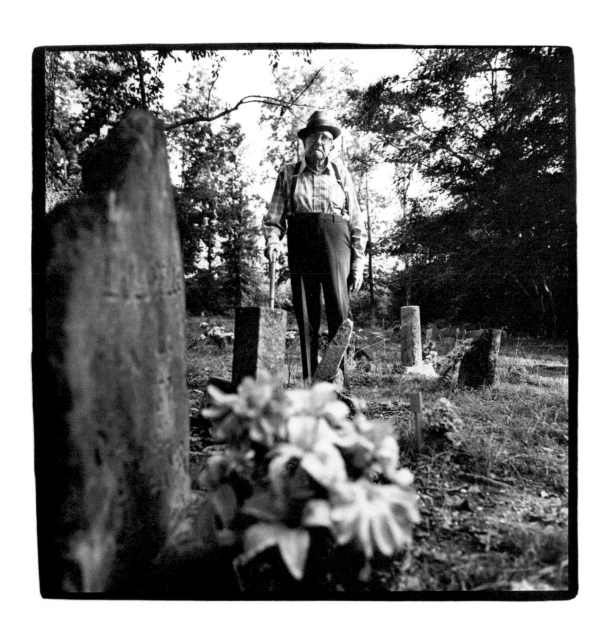

Amos Powers
TOUR GUIDE, KEY UNDERWOOD COON DOG MEMORIAL GRAVEYARD
COLBERT COUNTY, ALABAMA

There's just one surefire way to find the Key Underwood Coon Dog Memorial Graveyard, buried deep within the Freedom Hills of Colbert County, Alabama: track down Mr. Amos Powers of nearby Vina, Alabama. The eighty-six-year-old retiree is always a willing guide to this one-of-a-kind cemetery. "This is it," Powers rasps, when we finally arrive. "The coon dog graveyard. Only graveyard of its kind in the world . . . far as we know."

The graveyard sits in a clearing at the end of a long gravel road. The small plot of land is crowded with tombstones: "Black Ranger: He was good as the best and better than the rest." "Rusty: A coon dog indeed!" Old Tip . . . Old Lou . . . Rough . . . Ranger . . . Small bundles of plastic flowers lie beside each stone. "Troop's the first coon dog that was buried here back in 1937," Powers explains as he leads me to Troop's stone beside an old pine tree. "Best in the country at that time. Friendly dog. Good nose. Good voice. Story's told that he treed three different coons up the same tree in one night. That's a good dog! Belonged to a fella Tom Hall. He let the moonshiner H. E. Files have the dog. H. E. Files got caught making whiskey and went to penitentiary. When Files went to

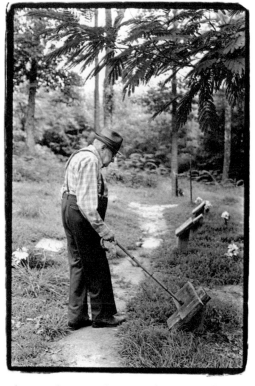

penitentiary his wife sold Troop to Key Underwood. He's the one that owned Troop when he died. The night he died, Key Underwood mentioned, 'We need to bury Old Troop at the pine tree.' This was his favorite place to hunt. They brought him over here and buried him three foot deep. That night. So that's the beginning. Boy, a lot of history here. . . . If I could just remember it all!"

William Bolton is also at the cemetery on this rather foreboding afternoon, raking leaves. Bolton is the graveyard's caretaker, as well as secretary and treasurer of the Tennessee Valley Coon Hunters Association. He's been associated with the cemetery since the 1940s. "We have some pretty strict rules you got to abide by here when you bury your dog here," Bolton explains. "You can't bury nothing but a full-blooded coon hound—can't be a house dog! And somebody besides the

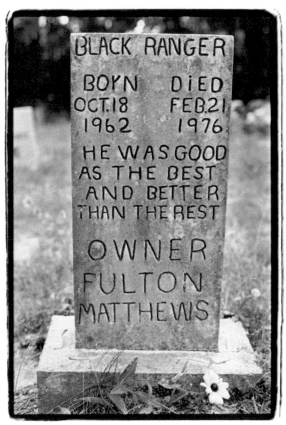

BLACK RANGER

BORN   DiED
OCT.18   FEB.21
1962   1976

HE WAS GOOD
AS THE BEST
AND BETTER
THAN THE REST

OWNER
FULTON
MATTHEWS

owners got to confer that this dog is a real good dog. And an officer's supposed to see the dog before you bury it. Some people think they might slip out here and bury a house dog, see, and we have a lot of problems with that. But this wouldn't be worth nothing if you let everybody bury every kind of a dog here.

"My dog is this one up here," Bolton says, as we approach the final resting place of a coon dog named Red. "I've had a lot of coon dogs in a lifetime, and . . . uh . . . I do miss him." Bolton begins to weep. "Standing here brings back quite a bit of memories."

"A good coon dog," Amos Powers explains softly, "is like one of the family." We leave William Bolton alone with Red, and wander among the gravestones. ∎

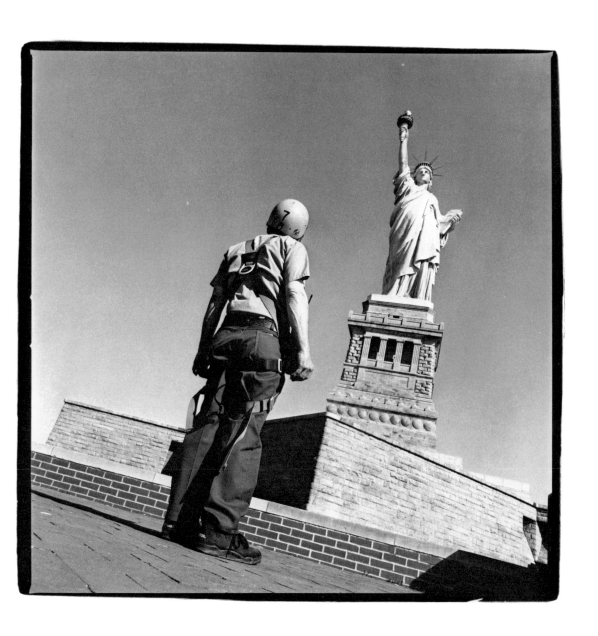

Charlie DeLeo
MAINTENANCE MAN, STATUE OF LIBERTY
NEW YORK CITY

Charlie DeLeo is the Statue of Liberty's caretaker. His official title is Maintenance Mechanics Helper, but since the early seventies Charlie's been known as "the keeper of the flame"—the man responsible for the upkeep of the statue's torch and crown.

Each morning, before the tourists arrive, Charlie climbs up Lady Liberty's arm and makes his way out onto the catwalk surrounding her torch. He cleans and polishes, and, if necessary, changes the bulbs which light the flame at night. Then he heads back down the arm to clean the twenty-five windows in the statue's crown. When he's finished, Charlie remains in the crown by himself meditating, praying, or talking to the statue. When the first tourists of the morning arrive, breaking his solitude, Charlie heads down to join the other maintenance workers in the more conventional day-to-day tasks involved in the monument's upkeep.

I interviewed Charlie early one morning in 1989 at the statue's crown. When I met him, Charlie lived alone in a small apartment in Brooklyn and donated most of his salary to charity.

I first came here when I was nine years old with my fourth-grade classmates. I remember we were going up to the crown, and it was like being in a spaceship. When we got to the top of the crown I asked the teacher, "Could we go in the arm?" She said, "No, the arm is closed." And I was so disappointed. Little did I know that my destiny would be to someday take care of that torch I so badly wanted to go into.

I've been working here since March of 1972, when I took a ferryboat ride on the Circle Line. I was out of work at the time, and chanced to see my favorite gal in New York Harbor. Halfway over I got an inspiration to ask for a job. When I got to the island I was hired as a temporary maintenance man. A few months later I became permanent.

At that time, no one was taking care of the torch officially. Different people would go up there to change lightbulbs, but very seldom was any real maintenance work done. So I started to go up on my own. I was washing the inside of the glass flame—the two hundred little windowpanes—and changing lightbulbs. My superiors realized, "Here's a guy that not only doesn't complain about the height or the climb, but is willing to work out on the girders!" (that's the superstructure that holds the statue together). Before you know it, they made me full-time caretaker of the torch.

I've seen it all here—bomb threats, demonstrations. One time a couple of years ago I was outside, and all of a sudden I heard noises and I looked up to the top of the statue, and the crown's windows were being busted and knocked down. I got excited and told one of the rangers, "Hey, somebody's smashing the windows in the crown." So I ran up there. No elevator. And I got almost to the top, huffing and puffing, and a woman jumps down—an Iranian woman—and she shoves me out of the way and tells me, "Get out of here! Go back! This is none of your business!" And I shoved her out of the way. I was ready to jump in the crown when another Iranian—a man—jumped down. He had a cold chisel, and he was trying to hit me with it and kick me in the face at the same time. I was a little scared—I didn't know what was happening. There were four others that were breaking windows—cold chisels and hammers. I told them, "Would you please stop it?" They wouldn't stop. They wanted to put their banners up. It was an awful experience—it was like somebody was attacking my own mother. When they finally stopped I felt kind of like I let the statue down, since I didn't overwhelm them, but then I realized I couldn't overwhelm six people. I mean, that woman alone looked like a weight lifter.

It's a feeling of peace and solitude up here, and an awareness of God's presence. To me this is like a little chapel in New York Harbor. I like to sing songs up here (not when people are around—I got a horrible voice.) I like to pray for America and for other countries—for everybody who longs to breathe the sweet fresh air of liberty. I compose poems up here too. I could picture the young King David, when he was a shepherd writing his psalms—that's how I feel. A lot of my best poems have come from inspirations from the torch.

You know, I'm the only man in history ever to stand on top of the golden flame. The first one and the only one. It's like being the first man on top of Mount Everest. It's a fantastic feeling. Some people think I'm a little crazy. How many guys stand on top of the golden flame of Liberty or on the superstructure where you've got hundred-foot drops? I don't look at it as me being a little crazy. I'm a true caretaker. Like Quasimodo was to Notre Dame, Charlie DeLeo is to Lady Liberty. Period! And he had no second thoughts about scaling the outside of the cathedral, or ringing those massive bells, and I don't have any second thoughts about what I do. ■

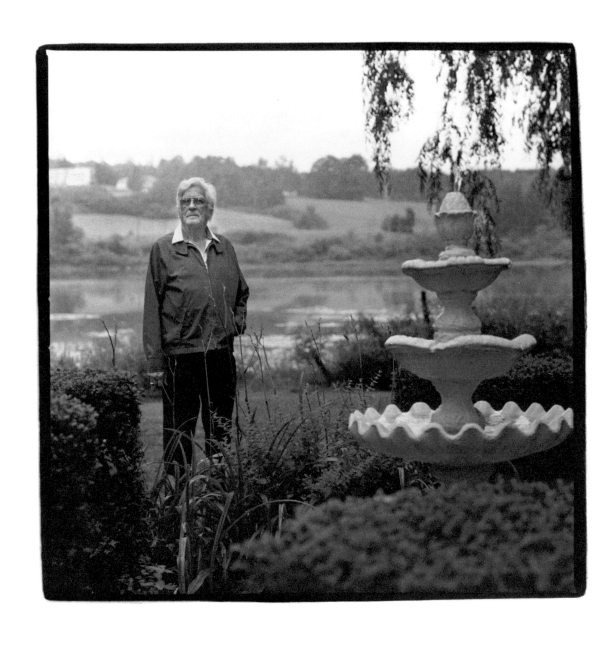

Joe Merrill and Hilda Wilkinson
SPIRITUALISTS
LILY DALE, NEW YORK

Lily Dale, New York, is the world capital of spiritualism. Located about fifty miles southwest of Buffalo, the community, founded in 1879, is home to some 250 year-round residents who subscribe to the belief that life continues after death and that spirits can communicate with the living through mediums. The modern spiritualist movement began in 1848 in Hydesville, New York (near Rochester), when two young sisters, Kate and Margaret Fox, were said to have heard rapping noises in their home, and found they could communicate with the presence by knocking back. Word of the Fox sisters spread, and organizations began cropping up across the country to advance the new religion of spiritualism. The Lily Dale Assembly was one of them.

Lily Dale is a lovely place to visit. A five-dollar gate fee admits visitors to the lakeside settlement. Picturesque turn-of-the century houses and cottages are packed close together on narrow tree-lined streets. Thousands of visitors pass through the community each summer, despite the fact that spiritualism has been in a steady decline since the early years of this century. The days when the streets of Lily Dale would be swarming with believers shuttling from one spectacular demonstration of psychic phenomena to the next are long gone. Indeed, Lily Dale is now largely dominated by New Agers. Books by Shirley MacLaine and Ram Dass take up most of the shelf space at the community bookstore. The featured event during the summer we visited was a lecture by Swami Beyondananda (who calls himself "the Yogi from Muskogee" and sports a large multicolored Afro), who was offering a weekend workshop: "The Lighter Side of Enlightenment: Swami's hilarious, uplifting comedy and his wife Trudy's heart-opening dance." This doesn't sit well with residents who remain from the golden age of spiritualism.

Harvey and I visited two of these senior members of the community in August 1993: Joe Merrill and Hilda Wilkinson. Hilda Wilkinson, who has been affiliated with Lily Dale for more than seventy years, initially refused our request for an interview and portrait. She said she'd been misquoted by the press too many times. After being barraged by a series of pleading letters from us, Hilda relented at the last moment—grudgingly. We ended up spending most of our day at Lily Dale with Hilda, who talked to us, fed us, and toured us around. Joe Merrill, who was ninety years old when we met him, holds the office of president of the National Spiritualist Association of Churches.

JOE MERRILL

My name is Joseph H. Merrill—I use the H. in the middle, I guess for my own satisfaction. I was born in Norway, Maine, and I became interested in spiritualism when I was a junior in high school. I was having breakfast one Sunday morning, and my mother said, "Joe, how would you like to go to a spiritualist meeting with me tonight?" I said, "Yeah, I'd love it." So I went that Sunday, and then I went Wednesday, and after I had been going to spiritualist meetings for a few months I joined the spiritualist church.

Spiritualism is a philosophy of life proving that there is no death, and that the life force of the individual continues. How did spiritualism begin? It started with the "rappings" that the Fox family heard. They heard them all over their house— sometimes in the wall, sometimes in the ceiling, sometimes in the floor. Naturally it bothered the family. The two young children, Katie and Margaret, in their childish ways said, "Let's try to talk to them." And they found that they could by snapping their fingers. If they snapped once, they'd hear one rap. If they snapped twice, they'd hear two raps. Finally they found that they could carry on a conversation. And in the rappings they were told that there was a peddler that had been murdered in that house, and that his body was in the cellar. And down in the basement they found the skeleton of the peddler and the peddler's pack that he carried.

That peddler's pack is now in the museum of the Lily Dale Library. And many, many years ago a man transported the house that the Foxes lived in from Hydesville up here to East Street. The house burned in 1935. I went many times to that house. Floy Cotrell was the medium who lived there, and they called her "the rapping medium." You could go into the house, and you could sit there and you'd hear the raps on the wall, on the ceiling and on the floor, and she gave you the opportunity of asking questions that could be answered "yes" or "no" or "doubtful" with the raps. And you could sit there and carry on a conversation with whoever you wanted to talk to from spirit. That was an actual happening!

Back then we had materialization mediums. We had levitation mediums—a table might rise with people standing around it. We had slate-writing. Frank Slater lived here, and he was a noted slate writing medium. He would put a slate somewhere and spirit would write a message on the slate. We had trumpet mediums, where spirit would speak through the trumpet. The trumpet would be floating around, and the spirit would give you a message. I've got a trumpet upstairs I could show you.

I had a friend whose mother had passed away one September. In October we were privileged to sit in a materializing séance—the medium was Millicent Benedict. We were sitting there, and all of a sudden I felt a nudge. And I said to my friend, "Somebody wants to grow here!" You won't believe this and very few people would, but I saw it with my own eyes, so I know. I saw a white substance about the size of a golf ball, and it started to grow. It grew to the size of a balloon, and as it grew it took on arms and features and a head. And that was a woman, and she put her arm around my friend—and it was his mother who had passed away just a month before that! I saw that with my own eyes!

Now we've got what they call "the New Age." There's nothing new about the New Age. It's just a new way of presenting the old thoughts. Mediumship in the early days was far more evidential than it is today. Today, people will get a shiver up their back, go hang a shingle out and say they're a medium. But it's not the mediumship of the old days!

HILDA WILKINSON

I'm Hilda Wilkinson and right now I'm eighty-eight—I'll be eighty-nine in a few weeks. I first came to Lily Dale on July 7, 1922. It was on a weekend, a Friday or Saturday, and the first time I came through the gates I thought, "Oh, how great Thou art! What a beautiful place to live." And it is!

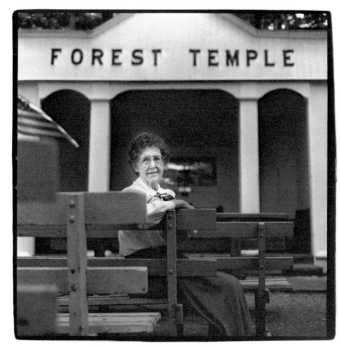

I grew up in spiritualism. I had a sister who was a born medium. Entities spoke through her body. I was about nine years old when I first became aware. We were kids, you know. There was four of us at home, getting ready for Sunday school. I was up and ready, and my sister was still in bed. All of a sudden I run out into the kitchen and I said to my mother, "Julia's talking like a man!" So Mother comes into the bedroom, and the voice said, "Don't be alarmed. She is a born medium, and she will do great work!" That opened our eyes to spiritualism. That was before the First World War.

That was the state of physical mediumship then. Was trance, was trumpet, materialization, psychometry, billet reading—all that sort of thing. It's sort of worn itself out now. We had Jack Kelly, who was a blindfold billet reader. Three blindfolds on, and he'd wander through the audience and call out the answers to the questions people wrote on their billets. That has all faded out now. Now they just ask 'em, "Do you have a brother? Do you have a grandmother?" To me it's a big letdown to my intelligence. In those days, we had *real* psychic phenomena and *real* spiritualism. We had people here all up and down our streets—it was like a parade it was so crowded. Still, it was all hush-hush. I wouldn't dare go to work on Monday morning and tell people where I was—I'd be afraid I wouldn't have a job. Now it's in the open, which is a good thing.

Spiritualism is as old as time. Just go back to Joan of Arc. She heard the voices. That's the way I look at it. Can you accept birth and rebirth? That you can come back to earth again? Are you familiar with Ella Wheeler Wilcox—the greatest lady of our time? She wrote poetry. She wrote:

> From body to body your spirit speeds on.
> It seeks a new form when the old one is gone.
> And the form that it finds is the fabric you wrought
> on the loom of the mind with the fiber of thought.

You were and you will be. Know this while you are. Now think about that! ■

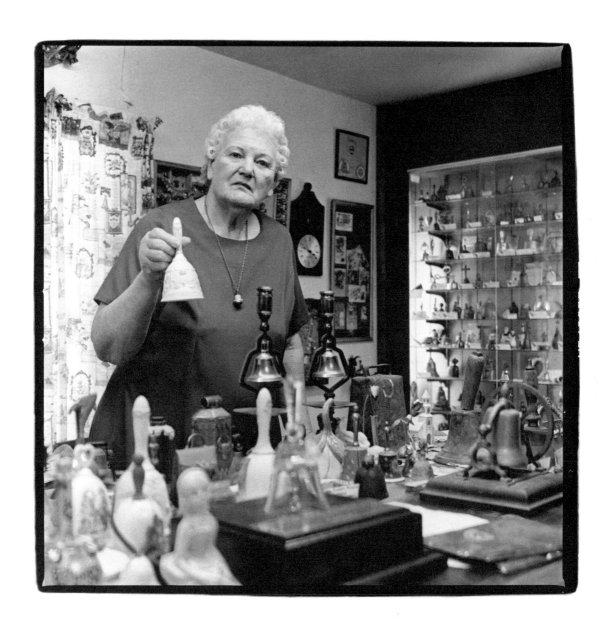

Virginia Belle Brewer
CURATOR, BREWER'S BELL MUSEUM
CANTON, TEXAS

I was due to show up at Brewer's Bell Museum at the end of a long reporting trip through Texas. I was exhausted, with only a couple of hours to spare before my plane was to take off out of Dallas. My schedule read: "11/23 A.M.: Virginia Brewer has a bell museum at the back of her house. Really not sure about this story. Probably forget it." I called her that morning and told her I was sorry, but I didn't have time to visit. I wished her the best of luck. She sounded sad. Really sad. I called her back and told her I'd drop by for a few minutes, cursing myself for being such a softy. I wasn't in the mood to talk to her. At all. I was anxious about missing my plane. I showed up, and, as I'll sometimes do in similar situations, I strapped on my recorder and pretended to tape without ever turning on the machine. She began showing me her bells. I was thoroughly underwhelmed, and began rushing her through the museum. As we stood in front of a cowbell from Bali she launched into the story of her museum, of how she'd given up everything for her bells. I froze. I switched on my tape recorder, and asked her to please start again from the beginning. She did. It was one of the most powerful moments of the three years I spent traveling on this project. I stayed with Ms. Brewer for about an hour, and made it to my plane with minutes to spare.

My name is Virginia Belle Brewer, and right now we're at Brewer's Bell Museum in Canton, Texas. I've been collecting bells for fifty-two years. Started in the fall of 1940. My sister Helen came in with a Tiffin crystal bell, and said, "This is a gift of a lifetime to come." Little did she realize what she was starting! To date I have three thousand, two hundred and thirty different bells from all fifty states and seventy-six countries. When people say, "Which is your favorite bell?" I say, "How many children do you have?" You just don't have a favorite! It's just not right.

I opened this museum in May 1973. All the time I was collecting everybody said, "What are you going to do with the bells?" And then I started to think, "Yes . . . a bell museum!" There was no other bell museum in Texas, so I thought people would start flocking in. Well, it didn't work out the way I anticipated. I opened the doors . . . but the people didn't come to see the bells.

They usually say a business starting has to take care of itself at first. I gave it four or five years. Still, nobody came. Then I decided that I'd have to buckle down and I'd have to start saving every way I could. So, one by one by one, I did without. Things that I thought was important, was necessities, I found you can live without them if you have to. . . . Like going on food stamps. That was very hard to do. But I had to do it. So, it's just one of those things!

I'm sorry to say, I still don't have many visitors here. It's very discouraging to open at nine o'clock, and then close up at six, and nobody comes. Got a little dog—Sessie Belle. She watches the parking lot for me and tells me when somebody drives up. I had two last week. A couple came. And that was it. . . . It's lonely back here, but when someone's with me and I can tell them some of the stories behind the bells, well then the bells come alive, and I come alive!

It's two dollars for adults and one dollar for children. You get a conducted tour of the museum, I play the musical handbells, answer questions about the unusual bells. When I tell people it takes an hour, they think I'm crazy. But when they get in the back room they say, "I could spend all day in here!" Then people say, "Oh, but you're taking your time." I say, "Well, the Lord gives me my time, and I have to spend it the way the Lord wants me to spend it. And I think this is it."

It's just a small museum—two rooms and a hall crowded completely with bells. And the old house is falling down on me. When I had that bad flu last year the wind blew the covering off my roof, so there's lots of mold and mildew everywhere, and that brings my asthma spells on. I'm not happy with this old house. I wish it would be torn down, so there could be a new home for the bells.

I've got a great big dream that the bells will be housed permanently somewhere, because with my asthma I may not make it through the night. I never know. Never did get married or have any children, so I want to leave my bells to posterity, where they can be seen all the time. My one requirement is for them not to be sold. Selling one at a time would be horrible. It would break up the family. I would haunt anybody that sold them!

I feel like the Lord intended me to share the beauty of bells with others. When the time comes, I feel He'll work things out so the bells can be carried on long, long, long after I'm gone. That gives me the steam to keep on keeping on. I wish it could have been easier. . . . But, I gotta keep on. ■

Appendix

"STEAM TRAIN" MAURY GRAHAM Interview: 8/92 (Britt, Iowa). Photograph: 7/93 (Logansport, Indiana). Aired on All Things Considered 9/92.

LAWRENCE DAVIS Interview: 9/92. Photograph: 1/94. Aired on Weekend All Things Considered 3/94.

ROBERT SHIELDS Interview: 10/93. Photograph: 10/93. Aired on Morning Edition 1/94.

MOREESE BICKHAM Interview: 2/90. Photograph: 6/92. "Tossing Away the Keys" aired on Weekend All Things Considered and Soundprint 4/90.

MILES MAHAN Interview: 6/93. Photograph: 7/93. Aired on All Things Considered 7/93.

ROBERTA BLACKGOAT Interview: 6/93. Photograph: 7/93.

LOUIS H. GREVING Interview: 8/92. Photograph: 10/92. Aired on Weekend All Things Considered 9/92.

GENEVA TISDALE Interview and photograph: 10/93. Aired on Weekend All Things Considered 10/93.

HAROLD C. COTTON Interview: 10/93. Photograph: 12/93 (rephotographed).

PROPHET BLACKMON Interview: 8/92. Photograph: 10/92. Aired on Weekend All Things Considered 2/93.

TOMMIE BASS Interview: 11/91. Photograph: 7/92. Aired on All Things Considered 1/93.

DONALD BEAN Interview: 11/92. Photograph: 1/93. Aired on Morning Edition 5/93.

SYLVIA RIVERA AND SEYMOUR PINE Interviews: 4/89 and 7/94. Photograph: 7/94. "Remembering Stonewall" aired on Pacifica Radio and Weekend All Things Considered 6/89.

MACKEY E. BROWN Interview and photograph: 11/93.

DIXIE EVANS Interview: 6/93. Photograph: 12/92.

DICK FALK Interview and photograph: 9/91. Story on Airplane Ashes aired on Morning Edition 7/91.

SEGUNDO MUGARRA Interview: 6/93. Photograph: 8/93. Aired on Morning Edition 12/93.

DEWEY CHAFIN AND BARBARA ELKINS Interview: 5/92. Photograph: 9/92. "They Shall Take up Serpents" aired on Soundprint 9/92 and All Things Considered 11/92.

LESLIE KORFELD AND JOE ERBER Interview: 11/91. Photograph: 7/92. Aired on All Things Considered 12/91.

JAMES SMITH Interview and photograph: 8/93.

JIM SEARLES Interview: 5/90. Photograph: 7/94. Aired on Morning Edition 5/90.

HINKLE SCHILLINGS AND SHADE PATE Interview: 11/92. Photograph: 1/93. Aired on All Things Considered 2/93.

MARIE COOMBS Interview and photograph: 11/93.

MARTA BECKET AND TOM WILLETT Interview 6/93. Photograph: 7/93. Aired on Morning Edition 10/93.

Appendix

DAN FIELD Interview: 2/90. Photograph: 10/94. Aired on Weekend All Things Considered 2/90.

HALLIE STILLWELL Interview and photograph: 11/93.

PERCY BRIGHAM Interview: 10/93 (Umitilla Indian Reservation). Photograph: 6/94 (Cascade Locks, Ore.).

DICK ZIMMERMAN Interview and photograph: 11/93. Aired on All Things Considered 12/93.

LYDIA EMERY Interview and photograph: 10/93.

STANLEY KILARR Interview and photograph: 10/93.

MARION WALKER Interview and photograph: 11/93.

GEORGE PRESTON Interview: 8/92. Photograph: 10/92. Aired on Morning Edition 11/92.

Z. L. HILL Interview: 11/91. Photograph: 3/95. Aired on Morning Edition 4/92.

JIM BISHOP Interview and photograph: 11/93. Aired on All Things Considered 2/94.

MATT KENNEDY Interview: 6/90. Photograph: 7/94. Aired on Weekend All Things Considered 8/90.

MARIANO AND CLARA LUCCA Interview and photograph: 8/93. Aired on Morning Edition 10/93.

MIKE GASHWAZRA Interview: 6/93. Photograph: 7/93.

DAN BARLOW Interview: 6/93. Photograph: 7/93.

EVANGELINE CALVIN Interview and photograph: 10/93.

DR. HEPCAT Interview: 11/92. Photograph: 1/93. Aired on Weekend All Things Considered 1/94.

BILL SEWARD Interview and photograph: 11/93.

JOE FRANKLIN Interview: 8/91. Photograph: 7/93. Aired on Weekend All Things Considered 8/91.

FRED BLOODGOOD Interview: 8/92. Photograph: 10/92. Aired on Weekend All Things Considered 9/92.

AUGUSTINA MARTÍNEZ Interview and photograph: 11/93.

JOHNNY TOCCO Interview: 6/93. Photograph: 7/93.

AMOS POWERS Interview: 11/91. Photograph: 6/92. Aired on Weekend all Things Considered 10/92.

CHARLIE DELEO Interview: 7/89. Photograph: 4/94. Aired on Weekend All Things Considered 7/89.

JOE MERRILL AND HILDA WILKINSON Interviews and photographs: 8/93.

VIRGINIA BELLE BREWER Interview: 11/92. Photograph: 1/93. Aired on All Things Considered 12/92.

In most cases, the oral histories in *Holding On* are heavily edited transcripts of interviews which ranged in length from one to four hours.